This is the night of Hallowe'en
When all the witches might be seen;
Some of them black, some of them green,
Some of them like a turkey bean.

God bless the master of this house,
And its good mistress too,
And all the little children
That round the table go;
And all your kin and kinsmen,
That dwell both far and near;
We wish you a merry Christmas
And a happy New Year.

CHILDREN'S GARDEN

English for
Early Childhood Care and Education Majors

NAOKO AKAMATSU

SEIBIDO

音声ファイルのダウンロード／ストリーミング

CD Self-Study 自習用 CD マーク表示がある箇所は、音声を弊社 HP より無料でダウンロード／ストリーミングすることができます。トップページのバナーをクリックし、書籍検索してください。書籍詳細ページに音声ダウンロードアイコンがございますのでそちらから自習用音声としてご活用ください。

https://www.seibido.co.jp

Acknowledgment

Our special thanks to Ms. Yoko Sekine for her excellent illustrations, Urim, Gloria, Sam and Shimon for their sweet voices, and Chino for her good musical accompaniment.

Our thanks to the Penguin Group (USA) Inc. for permission to print the cover of *Good Night Gorilla* by Peggy Rathmann on page 37.

Children's Garden

Copyright © 2008 by Naoko Akamatsu

All rights reserved for Japan.
No part of this publication may be reproduced in any form
without permission from Seibido Co., Ltd.

PREFACE

Welcome to CHILDREN'S GARDEN!

CHILDREN'S GARDEN is an English course designed specifically for Early Childhood Education (ECE) and Childcare majors at vocational schools, colleges or universities. It offers practice in the type of English ECE students need when they work in an international setting with young children.

In my first English textbook *Childcare English*, I had the readers experience childcare and education through the eyes of a teacher at a Japanese nursery school. In this textbook, readers will vicariously experience an internship through the eyes of a peer at an international nursery school. This approach helps the Japanese ECE majors relate to the text.

This textbook emphasizes the development of communicative skills in the English language through authentic dialogues, model conversations and substitution drills. Exercises include: Listening comprehension, grammar and translation activities.

The model conversations are short, yet contain ample opportunities for students to practice and make use of their knowledge and experiences of nursery school or kindergarten education. The grammar exercises focus on selected areas of difficulty for Japanese learners (articles, tenses, prepositions, etc.). Attractive illustrations enliven each unit and provide students with visual images that will keep them motivated and involved.

Most units contain songs, rhymes, fingerplays, handicrafts and childcare information. These useful tips will help students to interact effectively with young children. In addition, singing rhymes can help students significantly improve their pronunciation and capture the rhythm of the English language.

Finally, I would like to thank Mrs. Waltraud Oka who was instrumental in creating the exercises and reviewing the English. I would also like to thank Professor Keiko Kishii who provided background information on preschool education from a professional point of view. Ms. Yuri Komatsu also gave me valuable advice on childcare. I must also thank my students for their insights and encouragement.

Naoko Akamatsu

はしがき

　本書は、保育や幼児教育、児童福祉を学ぶ学生のために「聞く」「話す」「読む」「書く」を効果的に学習できるように作成した総合教材です。外国の子どもたちが日本の子どもたちと共に育ち、遊び、学ぶChildren's Gardenという国際的な保育園がテキストの舞台です。実習生加藤えみさんがこの園を事前訪問するところからお話が始まります。実習を通して成長していく一人の学生の貴重な体験が教材になりました。学生の皆さんも、きっと、興味深く読み進められることでしょう。

　本書は実習前のオリエンテーションから実習後の再訪までの場面を全12章で構成し、効果的に楽しく学習できるように、学習課題を絞り各章を6つのセクションに分けました。

本書の使い方

1. **Judging from Pictures:** 各章のテーマに関連したイラストを見ながら質問に答え、また、ペアになって意見交換をします。選択問題でイラスト上のアイテムを表現する語句を学習します。このウォームアップは、次のリスニング教材を理解するための準備になります。

2. **Listening Comprehension:** リスニングに必要なキーワード、キーフレーズを日本語訳とのマッチング形式で学習します。イラストからもリスニングの内容を想像できます。CDをよく聴いたあとに、リスニングの内容把握を正誤問題でチェックします。

3. **Advice for the Internship:** えみが講義ノートに書きとめた基本的な実習の心得、実習園に関する情報、実習生へのアドバイスなどが平易な英文で書かれています。語句の補足説明を手がかりに英文の流れに沿って内容を理解しながら和訳します。

    Talking to Children: 子どもたちへの声かけに役立つ文例を英訳します。単語を並び替え、英文を完成させます。口語的な短文を作成します。

4. **Conversation:** CDの会話を聞き、穴埋めや選択問題を通して、関連語句や表現を習得します。役割練習をするときは、感情をこめて発話しましょう。さらに、語句を入れ替えながら、別の英語表現を学習する発展ドリルを繰り返し練習できます。

5. **Reading and Listening:** えみの日記を読みます。実習中のエピソードが満載です。穴埋めや選択問題を通して、基礎的な文法、語法の復習をします。内容把握は、三択問題でチェックします。最後にクイズや雑学・豆知識紹介があります。気軽に読んで楽しみましょう。

6. **Good Time with Nursery Rhymes:** 実際に園児たちと楽しめる実践的な手遊び唄をはじめ、なぞなぞ、子守唄、詩歌などを紹介しています。マザーグースを唄うことは英語の発音、イントネーション、リズムの練習になります。大きな声で音読練習しましょう。また、紙コップのおもちゃ、お菓子の家など、簡単に製作でき、子どもたちと一緒に遊べるクラフトを紹介しています。インストラクションを和訳し、製作してみましょう。ここからも保育的に役立つアイデアがたくさん汲み取れるでしょう。

CONTENTS

Chapter 1   **Children's Garden** "I Start My First Internship Next Month." 6
こどもの園保育園 "来月、実習が始まります"

Chapter 2   **The First Day of the Internship** "I'm Emi Kato, a Student Teacher." 12
実習初日 "実習生の加藤えみです"

Chapter 3   **Out We Go!** "Children, It's a Nice Day." 18
さあ、出かけましょう！ "いいお天気ね"

Chapter 4   **Splish, Splash** "Like an Olympic Swimmer." 24
バシャバシャ、水しぶき "オリンピック選手みたい"

Chapter 5   **Pancake Day** "Yum, Yum, Yummy!" 30
ホットケーキの日 "おいしい、おいしい、おいしいよ"

Chapter 6   **Read Me, Tell Me Stories** "What Story are You Reading Us?" 36
本を読んで、お話を聞かせて "今日は何のお話？"

Chapter 7   **Activities with Watermelons** "A Watermelon Grows in My Tummy." 42
すいかで遊ぼう "おなかですいかが大きくなるよ"

Chapter 8   **Happy Birthday!** "A Star Was Born." 48
お誕生日おめでとう "スターが生まれました"

Chapter 9   **Children at Play** "Way to Go, Mark!" 54
子どもと遊び "マークくん、やったー！"

Chapter 10   **Baby News** "May I Change Her Diaper?" 60
赤ちゃんニュース "おむつ交換をしてもよろしいですか？"

Chapter 11   **The Tooth Fairy** "She Leaves Money Under the Pillow." 68
歯の妖精 "枕の下にお金を置いてくれるの"

Chapter 12   **The Green-Eyed Witch** "Which Witch Watched Which Watch?" 72
緑の目の魔女 "どの魔女がどの時計を見たの？"

Grammar Notes 78

References 86

1 CHILDREN'S GARDEN
"I Start My First Internship Next Month."

1 JUDGING FROM PICTURES The School Brochure

Look at the pictures. Then read the questions and discuss the answers.

a) Where is this? Have you been to a place like this? How old were you then?
b) What can you see? What are the children doing?
c) What kind of program does Children's Garden offer?

CHILDREN'S GARDEN NURSERY SCHOOL

We offer quality childcare and preschool education programs for infants, toddlers, and preschoolers that nurture the individual needs and abilities of each child.

Childcare Program

Classrooms	Group Size
Bambi Babies	10 infants
Duckling Ones	14 toddlers
Kitten Twos	16 children

Preschool Program

Classrooms	Group Size
Frog Threes	20 children
Ladybug Fours	20 children
Butterfly Fives	20 children

Program Times
Regular Program   8:00 a.m. - 5:30 p.m.
Extended Program 7:30 a.m. - 6:00 p.m.

---

school brochure 園のしおり、パンフレット   offer 提供する   quality 質の高い   childcare 保育
preschool education 就学前教育、幼児教育   nurture 育てる、はぐくむ   individual 個々の   ability 能力

2 LISTENING COMPREHENSION Emi's Self-introduction

Match the English and Japanese expressions.

1. major in   _____   a. 保育士/幼稚園教諭
2. early childhood education   _____   b. 専攻する
3. preschool teacher   _____   c. 履歴書
4. internship   _____   d. 実習
5. CV (curriculum vitae, resume)   _____   e. 幼児教育

Emi's CV

Family Name: Kato
First Name: Emi
Address & Zip Code: 132 Sakuramachi, Kita-ku, Tokyo 107-6002
Home Telephone: 503-4678-1239
Date of Birth: June 16, 1989
Nationality: Japanese
Sex: Female
Marital Status: Single
Work: Day-care Center Assistant (weekends only)
Education: Tokyo Junior College (sophomore)
Skills: Proficient in computers, English
Interests: Playing the piano, watching movies, skiing

Listen to the CD and check true (T) or false (F). 🎧 2

		T	F
1.	Emi is a third-year student.	☐	☐
2.	Her major in college is English.	☐	☐
3.	She hopes to work with young children later.	☐	☐
4.	Her internship at Children's Garden starts tomorrow.	☐	☐
5.	Ms. Ota is Emi's college friend.	☐	☐

---

introduction 紹介   **marital status** 婚姻関係の有無   **skills** 技能、技術

3 ADVICE FOR THE INTERNSHIP
The Philosophy of Children's Garden 🎧 3

Translate the sentences into Japanese.

① Children's Garden is a special place for children to learn, play, and **socialize** [社会性をはぐくむ] in a happy, safe and nurturing environment.

② We welcome children from a variety of cultural backgrounds. We teach children to **respect** [尊重する] different cultures and ideas.

③ The teachers at Children's Garden are always patient and **supportive** [援助する]. They **interact** [触れ合う、関わる] with children by talking and listening to them.

TALKING TO CHILDREN
Useful Expressions for a First Interaction with Babies

Translate Japanese sentences into English, arranging the given words.

1. メアリーちゃん、あなたはお父さん似ね。(you, like, your, Mary, look, father)

   _____ .

2. やわらかいほっぺたね。(so, soft, your, cheeks, are)

   _____ .

3. 小さなおててにあんよだね。(feet, you, and, hands, such, have, tiny)

   _____ .

4. 抱っこしてほしいのね？(hold, me, you, do, you, to, want)

   _____ ?

---

philosophy 理念・方針

4 CONVERSATION Emi Meets Ms. Ota, the Head Teacher. 4

Fill in the blanks using the words in the box. Then listen to the CD and practice with your partner.

| a | an | any | my | our | some | your |

Emi: Hello, Ms. Ota. My name is Emi Kato. It's a pleasure to meet you.
Ota: It's a pleasure to meet you, too, Miss Kato. Please have 1)_____ seat.
Emi: Thank you. Here's 2)_____ CV.
Ota: Oh, yes. May I ask you 3)_____ questions?
Emi: Of course.
Ota: Where do you live?
Emi: I live in Tokyo.
Ota: How do you come to 4)_____ school?
Emi: I come by bus and train.
Ota: How long does it take?
Emi: About 5)_____ hour.
Ota: What do you do in 6)_____ free time?
Emi: I play the piano or watch movies. Well, I sometimes go shopping.
Ota: You speak good English. Have you been abroad?
Emi: Yes. I was lucky to have spent four years in Australia when I was little.
Ota: I see. Now, do you have 7)_____ questions?

PRACTICE

Walk around the room and ask two people the questions below. Write their answers.

Questions	Person 1	Person 2
1. What is your first name?	_____	_____
2. Where do you live?	_____	_____
3. How do you come to school?	_____	_____
4. How long does it take?	_____	_____
5. What do you do in your free time?	_____	_____
6. Have you been abroad?	_____	_____

head teacher 主任　時間の表現例：30 minutes = half an hour　90 minutes = an (one) hour and a half = one and a half hours

5 READING AND LISTENING Emi's Journal — Orientation

Read the journal entry and circle the correct words. Then listen to the CD. (See Grammar Notes on page 82)

Friday, May 12. About two weeks ago, I scheduled an orientation with Ms. Ota. I called during the children's nap time, which is between 1:30 pm and 2:30 pm, since the teachers are the ⁱ⁾ most / least busy during this hour. I knew I should be careful while speaking on the phone, so I spoke slowly and used the ²⁾ more / less formal manner of expressions.

   Today was orientation day. Ms. Ota explained their school's philosophy and gave me the school calendar. She is not only the head teacher, but also the five-year-olds' classroom teacher. She showed me around the school and let me observe all the classroom activities. I learned how the children spend their days at school.

   The ³⁾ best / worst thing about Children's Garden is that it will provide me with an opportunity to meet children from different backgrounds and cultures. My internship starts next month. I can't wait! Just a ⁴⁾ few / little more weeks to go!

Which of the answers are correct?

1. Emi _____ the children when she visited Children's Garden.
   a) taught
   b) played with
   c) saw

2. In Children's Garden, there are _____.
   a) no Japanese children.
   b) children of various nationalities.
   c) returnees only.

Q UIZ

Which words in the story mean the opposite of:

1. fast   ↔ _____
2. same   ↔ _____
3. careless ↔ _____
4. free   ↔ _____
5. casual   ↔ _____

---

nap time 昼寝の時間　formal 改まった　expression 表現、(ことばの) 言いまわし　explain 説明する
observe 見学する　provide 提供する　opportunity 機会、好機

6 FUN TIMES WITH NURSERY RHYMES 🎵6
Sing Nursery Songs and Enjoy a Fingerplay.

英語の手遊び唄をとおして、英語のリズム、発音、イントネーション、語彙を学習しましょう。
音読練習の後に唄ってみましょう。手遊びも練習してみましょう。

WHERE IS THUMBKIN?
("ARE YOU SLEEPING?" の替え歌)

① Where is <u>Thumbkin</u>?
① Where is <u>Thumbkin</u>?
② Here I am. Here I am.
③ How are you today, sir?
③ Very well, I thank you.
④ Run away. Run away.

① Hands behind back.

② Show one thumb, then the other.

③ Bend one thumb, then the other.

④ Wiggle one thumb away, then the other.

VARIATIONS

You can repeat using other fingers: Pointer (index finger)
Tall Man (middle finger)
Ring Man (ring finger)
Baby (little finger)

---

sir あなたさま（男性に対する敬称、日本語に訳さないことが多い）

2 THE FIRST DAY OF THE INTERNSHIP
"I'm Emi Kato, a Student Teacher."

1 JUDGING FROM PICTURES Play House

Look at the pictures. Then read the questions and discuss the answers.

a) What are the children doing? What do you think they are saying?
b) Did you play house when you were little? Where?
c) Which family member did you pretend to be?

Write the number of each item in the correct box.

| 1. stove | 2. refrigerator | 3. ladle | 4. rolling pin | 5. mixing bowl |
| 6. sink | 7. whisk | 8. cutting board | 9. teakettle | 10. spatula (turner) |

ANSWER: a ☐ b ☐ c ☐ d ☐ e ☐ f ☐ g ☐ h ☐ i ☐ j ☐

---

pretend to be 〜であるまねをして遊ぶ

2 LISTENING COMPREHENSION Emi Meets Ana, an American Child.

Match the English and Japanese expressions.

1. chin-up bar _____   a. つるつる滑る
2. wipe _____   b. 実習生
3. slippery _____   c. ふく、ふき取る
4. dangerous _____   d. 鉄棒
5. student teacher _____   e. 危ない

Listen to the CD and check true (T) or false (F). 🎧 7

	T	F
1. Emi speaks to Ana first.	☐	☐
2. Ana thinks Emi is a friend's mother.	☐	☐
3. It is raining again.	☐	☐
4. Ana doesn't want to help Emi.	☐	☐
5. Emi wants the children to play in a safe place.	☐	☐

3 ADVICE FOR THE INTERNSHIP
Emi's Lecture Notes — Internship Tips 🎧8

Translate the sentences into Japanese.

① Greet people **politely**(礼儀正しく) at the nursery school. Say a cheerful "Hello!" to everyone.

② Check the daily schedule with the classroom teacher first thing in the morning. This will **save you a hassle**(戸惑わないですむ).

③ Don't **tower over**(〜の上にそそり立つ) children. **Lower**(低くする) yourself to a child's level by bending down. Eye contact is very important.

TALKING TO CHILDREN
Useful Expressions for Interaction with Children at Nap Time

Translate Japanese sentences into English, arranging the given words.

1. 起きたかなあ。おめめが開いてるよ。(awake, are, open, your, eyes, you, are)

   _____? _____.

2. わあ、大きなあくびね。まだ、眠いの？ (yawn, you, big, are, wow, still, sleepy)

   _____! _____?

3. よく眠れたかなあ？ 暑かった？ (you, were, did, sleep, hot, you, well)

   _____? _____?

4. さあ、着替えましょうね。パジャマを脱いでね。(changed, okay, get, off, let's, pajamas, your, take)

   _____. _____.

---

lecture 講義　tip 助言、秘訣

4 CONVERSATION At the Chin-up Bars 🎧 9

Circle the correct words. Then listen to the CD and practice with your partner.

Emi: How ¹⁾tall / old are you, Ana?

Ana: I'm five.

Emi: Which ²⁾classroom / homeroom are you in?

Ana: I'm in ³⁾Firefly / Butterfly Fives. What school ⁴⁾do / are you go to?

Emi: I go to Tokyo Junior College.

Ana: Why are you here?

Emi: Because I want to be a ^a**preschool teacher** and I need to study how children ^b**play**. Let's ⁵⁾work / play together.

Ana: OK. Do you want to play ^c**house** ?

Emi: Sure!

SUBSTITUTION DRILL

Use the expressions below to make three more conversations like the one above.

a) Because I want to be a _____.

b) I need to study how children _____.

c) Do you want to play _____?

	a	b	c
	preschool teacher	play	house
1	kindergarten teacher	grow and develop	soccer
2	nursery school teacher	spend their days	hide and seek
3	childcare attendant	learn to get along with others	tag

---

nursery school teacher/preschool teacher 保育士   kindergarten teacher/ preschool teacher 幼稚園教諭   childcare attendant in a children's institution 児童養護施設職員

5 READING AND LISTENING
Emi's Journal — My First Day as an Intern 🔘 10

Read the journal entry and circle the correct words. Then listen to the CD. (See Grammar Notes on page 79)

Monday, June 5. When I arrived at Children's Garden, the rain ¹⁾stoped / stopped and the sun came out. Ms. Ota was standing at the gate. I greeted her with a polite and cheerful "Good morning, Ms. Ota." I had a good feeling that my first day would ²⁾go / went well.

I went to the locker room and ³⁾changed / changeed into a T-shirt and pants. I also wore an apron. Then I went back to Ms. Ota's classroom and checked the daily schedule. Ms. Ota was very nice. She told me I was free to ask questions anytime.

When I looked out of the window, I saw children ⁴⁾ran / running in the playground. I asked Ms. Ota, "May I go outside and wipe the chin-up bars? I think they are still wet." She ⁵⁾replyed / replied, "Yes, please. Thank you, Emi."

I took off my indoor shoes, put on my sneakers and went to the bars. While I was ⁶⁾wiped / wiping them with a cleaning cloth, a little girl ⁷⁾ran / running toward me. Her name was Ana and she ⁸⁾offered / offerred to help me. How nice!

Which of the answers are correct?

1. After Emi changed clothes, what did she do?
    a) She checked what the weather was like.
    b) She met Ms. Ota at the gate.
    c) She talked about the schedule with Ms. Ota.

2. Why did Emi go to the chin-up bars?
    a) Because she wanted to wipe them.
    b) Because Ms. Ota told her to wipe them.
    c) Because Ana asked her to wipe them.

Q UIZ

Which words in the story mean the same as:

1. young = _____
2. plan = _____
3. got to = _____
4. kind = _____
5. smoothly = _____

---

as an intern 実習生として　go well うまくいく　be free to~ 遠慮なく~する　anytime いつでも
may してよい　still まだ　reply 返事をする　take off 脱ぐ　put on 着る、身につける　toward の方へ

6 FUN TIMES WITH NURSERY RHYMES 🎧 11
Children Love Enchanting Rhymes and Rhythms.

英米国で古くから伝承されてきた童謡を総称してマザーグースMother Gooseと呼びます。子どもたちはマザーグースを耳にし、歌い、遊びながら成長します。手遊びが楽しめる遊び唄や、子守唄、なぞなぞ、占い、早口言葉など、その内容はバラエティに富んでいます。また、同じ韻を踏む、同韻語が使われている押韻詩がたくさんあります。きらきら星を歌いながら、押韻の面白さや英語の強弱のリズムを体験しましょう。

TWINKLE, TWINKLE, LITTLE STAR

① Twinkle, twinkle, little <u>star</u>,
② How I wonder what you _____!
③ Up above the world so <u>high</u>,
④ Like a diamond in the _____.
① Twinkle, twinkle, little <u>star</u>,
② How I wonder what you _____!

Can you find the rhymes for 'star' and 'high'? Choose the suitable words from the word lists and fill in the blanks in the song.

*star*の同韻語： are   bar   car   cigar   far   guitar   jar
*high*の同韻語： buy   eye   July   my   tie   sky   why

① Open and shut hands.
② Point to chin in wonder.
③ Point to sky.
④ Make a diamond shape with fingers.

wonder 〜かしらと思う   above より上に

3 OUT WE GO!
"Children, It's a Nice Day."

1 JUDGING FROM PICTURES A Map of the Area around the School

Look at the map. Then read the questions and discuss the answers.

a) Which are your favorite places? Why?
b) Is there any place you've never visited?
c) Where would you like to go on a date?

Write the number of each icon in the correct box.

| 1. hospital | 2. coffee shop | 3. post office | 4. library | 5. convenience store |
| 6. church | 7. flower shop | 8. ballet school | 9. supermarket | 10. hairdresser's |

ANSWER: a ☐ b ☐ c ☐ d ☐ e ☐ f ☐ g ☐ h ☐ i ☐ j ☐

2 LISTENING COMPREHENSION Emi Talks to Mark, an English Child.

Match the English and Japanese expressions.

1. yay   _____   a. カタツムリ
2. restroom   _____   b. トイレ、洗面所
3. the other way around _____ c. 探す
4. look for   _____   d. あべこべに
5. snail   _____   e. いいぞ、万歳

Listen to the CD and check true (T) or false (F). 🎧 12

		T	F
1.	Today they'll go for a walk in the zoo.	☐	☐
2.	Before the walk the children must go to the restroom.	☐	☐
3.	Mark puts Emi's shoes on his own feet.	☐	☐
4.	Emi helps Mark with his zipper.	☐	☐
5.	Mark carries snails in a plastic box.	☐	☐

3 ADVICE FOR THE INTERNSHIP
Emi's Lecture Notes — Going for a Walk CD 13

Translate the sentences into Japanese.

① Some children **spend**(費やす) 12 hours a day at a nursery school from the time they are born until they are six years old.

② So, going for a walk is a **precious**(貴重な、大切な) time for them. They can get to know the **area**((周辺)地域) around their school, and enjoy nature.

③ Going for a walk is a simple daily activity, but the children always **discover**(発見する) something new.

TALKING TO CHILDREN
Useful Expressions for Interaction with Crying Babies

Translate Japanese sentences into English, arranging the given words.

1. どうしたの？どこか痛いの？(wrong, hurt, you, what's, are)

   _____? _____?

2. 何が悲しいのかなあ、マーサちゃん？(so, is, Martha, sad, making, what, you)

   _____?

3. ひとりになるのは嫌なのよね。(right, don't, alone, being, you, like)

   _____?

4. よし、よし。寝ようね。(to, go, hush, hush, sleep)

   _____. _____.

4 CONVERSATION On the Way to the Park 📀 14

Fill in the blanks using the words in the box. Then listen to the CD and practice with your partners.

at	by	in	inside	on	out	to

Ota: Children, please listen. I want you to line up ¹⁾_____ twos and hold hands.

Emi: Mark, hold my hand, OK? Look ²⁾_____ ! A ᵃ**bicycle** is coming. Step aside.

Mark: Miss Kato, do we cross here?

Emi: Not yet, because the traffic light is red. Red is for "stop." Now the light has changed ³⁾_____ green. Let's cross carefully.

Mark: First, we look right, then we look left, then right again.

Emi: ᵇ**Well done**, Mark. You're a good boy.

Mark: I am. Miss Kato, my house is ᶜ**behind** this bakery.

Emi: Really? But we have to go straight. Sorry, we can't stop ⁴⁾_____.

Mark: Look! Such pretty flowers! We're ⁵⁾_____ the park!

Ota: Children, don't step ⁶⁾_____ the flower bed, OK? Stay ⁷⁾_____ the path.

SUBSTITUTION DRILL

Use the expressions below to make three more conversations like the one above.

a) A _____ is coming!

b) _____, Mark.

c) Miss Kato, my house is _____ this bakery.

	a	b	c
	bicycle	well done	behind
1	motorcycle	nice work	opposite
2	bus	good job	near
3	car	excellent	next to

---

step aside わきへ寄る　straight まっすぐに　path （庭、公園などの）散歩道、通り道

5 READING AND LISTENING
Emi's Journal — Into the World of Children 🎧 15

Read the journal entry and circle the correct prepositions. Then listen to the CD. (See Grammar Notes on page 83)

Thursday, June 8. This morning Ms. Ota took the children for a walk. The children started walking, when Ana suddenly stopped. I wondered why, but realized she was looking for tiny little ladybug larvae ¹⁾ <u>under / above</u> the sweet-smelling daphne trees.

The baby ladybugs were crawling ²⁾ <u>on / in</u> the leaves. They were black and orange and looked like miniature alligators. Ana told me those ugly baby ladybugs would become pupae, and then beautiful creatures in several weeks. She loves insects.

Mark and two other boys stopped to watch a steam shovel ³⁾ <u>at / for</u> a construction site. Ms. Ota understood their feelings and didn't hurry them. They took their time watching it dig a hole. When we came back to the school, the boys drew a picture ⁴⁾ <u>of / with</u> the steam shovel.

I learned that children express their newfound excitement not only in words but in their handiwork. It fascinates me to see the world ⁵⁾ <u>through / between</u> the eyes of children. I'm learning a lot ⁶⁾ <u>from / to</u> them.

Which of the answers are correct?

1. Ana stopped to...
   a) look at tiny alligators.
   b) study ladybug larvae.
   c) catch some ladybugs.

2. Emi thought Ms. Ota was wise because...
   a) she let the boys play with the steam shovel.
   b) she gave the boys some time to watch the steam shovel.
   c) she made the boys dig a hole with the steam shovel.

LET'S PLAY ANAGRAMS.

Make five words using the letters O-P-S-T.

....
....
....
....
....

---

larvae 幼虫（複数形）　**daphne** 沈丁花　**pupae** さなぎ（複数形）　**creature** 生き物　**steam shovel** ショベルカー　**construction site** 建設現場　**fascinate** 興味をそそる

6 FUN TIMES WITH NURSERY RHYMES 🎵 16
Children Love the Challenge of a Riddle.

マザーグースのなぞなぞ唄Humpty DumptyとLittle Nancy Etticoatを読んでみましょう。Humpty Dumptyはルイス・キャロルの「鏡の国のアリス」に登場するイラストが有名ですが、様々な絵本に、様々な卵のかたちをしたハンプティが描かれています。また、白いペチコートをはいているナンシー・エティコートさんとは、一体誰でしょう？なぞなぞを解いてみましょう。

HUMPTY DUMPTY

Humpty Dumpty sat on a wall.
Humpty Dumpty had a great fall.
All the king's horses and all the king's men
Couldn't put Humpty together again.

Answer the questions.

a) What happened to Humpty Dumpty? _____.
b) Who tried to help him? _____.
c) Was he put back together? _____.
d) What is Humpty Dumpty? _____.

Read the riddle rhyme and write the answer.

LITTLE NANCY ETTICOAT

Little Nancy Etticoat,
With a white petticoat,
And a red nose;
She has no feet or hands,
The longer she stands
The shorter she grows.

Who am I ?
Answer: _____.

---

riddle なぞなぞ　wall 塀　fall 落下　the king's men 王様の家来　put…together 組み立てる、よせ集める

4 SPLISH, SPLASH
"Like an Olympic Swimmer."

1 JUDGING FROM PICTURES Wading Pool

Look at the pictures. Then read the questions and discuss the answers.

a) What is going on here?
b) What are the children wearing or playing with?
c) What kind of water games did you play when you were little?

Write the number of each item in the correct box.

| 1. wading pool | 2. tub | 3. swimming cap | 4. whistle | 5. shovel |
| 6. inflatable tube | 7. bucket | 8. swimming trunks | 9. bikini | 10. swimsuit |

ANSWER: a [ ] b [ ] c [ ] d [ ] e [ ] f [ ] g [ ] h [ ] i [ ] j [ ]

---

wading pool 子ども用の浅いプール；ビニールプール

24

2 LISTENING COMPREHENSION Emi Has an Idea.

Match the English and Japanese words.

1. splash   _____   a. 探し、捜索、狩り
2. marbles   _____   b. なげる、ほうる
3. dive   _____   c. おはじき
4. hunt (n.) _____   d. はねかける、飛び散らす
5. toss   _____   e. ［水中に］潜る、飛び込む

Listen to the CD and check true (T) or false (F). 🎧 17

                                                                                 T   F

1. Emi tells Mark to stop splashing water on Ana.   ☐   ☐
2. Mark can swim underwater.   ☐   ☐
3. Ms. Ota is throwing marbles and coins into the pool.   ☐   ☐
4. Soyon doesn't feel safe in the water.   ☐   ☐
5. Emi finds a way to help Soyon.   ☐   ☐

3 ADVICE FOR THE INTERNSHIP   Emi's Lecture Notes — Water Play   CD 18

Translate the sentences into Japanese.

① Young children love playing with and in water. Playing with water makes them very excited.

② **Be aware** (認識している) that it only takes a second for children to lose their **footing** (足もと、足場). They can **drown** (溺死する) in less than **an inch** (2.54cm) of water.

③ Always watch them closely when they're in or near any water — a bucket, toilet, washing machine, bathtub, stream or lake.

TALKING TO CHILDREN
Useful Expressions for Interaction with Children at Free Playtime

Translate Japanese sentences into English, arranging the given words.

1. 私も仲間に入れてくれる？ 何をして遊ぼうか？(I, to, you, you, can, do, do, what, join, want)

   _____? _____?

2. 鬼ごっこ、縄跳び、それとも、一輪車に乗る？(play, unicycle, a, rope, tag, or, jump, ride)

   _____?

3. 外へ行って、ブランコで遊ぶのはどう？(outside, going, about, on, how, play, the, swing, to)

   _____?

4. 見て、ケイちゃんはあそこで積み木遊びしているね。(with, is, there, blocks, look, Kay, playing, over)

   _____.

4 CONVERSATION In the Water 🎧 19

Circle the correct words. Then listen to the CD and practice with your partner.

Emi: Soyon, do you ¹⁾<u>need / want</u> to put goggles on?

Soyon: Goggles?

Emi: Yes, goggles. They're just like glasses. You can open your eyes and ᵃ**see things** in the water when you wear goggles.

Soyon: Err...umm...OK, I'll put them on.

Emi: Ta-dah! You look just like an Olympic swimmer. You look ᵇ**cool**.

Soyon: ²⁾<u>Do / Would</u> I?

Emi: Soyon, look down and bend your ³⁾<u>knees / legs</u> slowly. Yes, yes, that's it. Good going! Look down there. Can you see the marbles? Can you reach them?

Soyon: Miss Kato, look! I've got three marbles.

Emi: Wow! You did it. That's ⁴⁾<u>terrible / terrific</u>. You're the ᶜ**winner**.

Soyon: Miss Kato, please ⁵⁾<u>save / hold</u> my marbles. I'll go get more.

Emi: Soyon, you ⁶⁾<u>kept / left</u> your goggles here. Don't forget your goggles!

SUBSTITUTION DRILL

Use the expressions below to make three more conversations like the one above.

a) You can open your eyes and _____ in the water.

b) You look _____.

c) You're the _____.

	a	b	c
	see things	cool	winner
1	put your face	perfect	champion
2	look for things	nice	star
3	be like a mermaid	fashionable	gold medalist

go get = go and get 取りに行く

5 READING AND LISTENING Emi's Journal — Children in the Water

Read the journal entry and put in the -ing forms of the verbs in the box. Then listen to the CD. (See Grammar Notes on page 81)

| touch | swim | scream | clap | wade | hold |

Friday, June 9. It was hot and humid. The children enjoyed cooling off in the 1)_____ pool, which I had filled with fresh water in the morning. Ms. Ota told them to take a shower before and after 2)_____. I told them not to swallow the water in the pool. The girls wore colorful bikinis and stylish one-piece suits. The boys wore swimming trunks. They were all very excited and kept 3)_____ in the water.

Ms. Ota got their attention by 4)_____ her hands. She introduced a new water game. She stood with her legs apart and let the kids swim through her legs. Some children made it through without 5)_____ her. Soyon, a Korean girl, practiced 6)_____ her breath. She was getting used to the water. Eventually she went through Ms. Ota's legs again and again.

The children also played a game where they dove for marbles at the bottom of the pool. Soyon shared her marbles with her friends who couldn't get any. How sweet! I was surprised to see that kind of caring behavior at an early age.

Which of the answers are correct?

1. What did Emi say to the children before they got into the pool?
   a) She warned them to be careful in the water.
   b) She warned them to save the water in the pool.
   c) She warned them not to drink the water.

2. What did Soyon do with her marbles?
   a) She gave them to Ms. Ota.
   b) She shared them with Emi.
   c) She shared them with her friends.

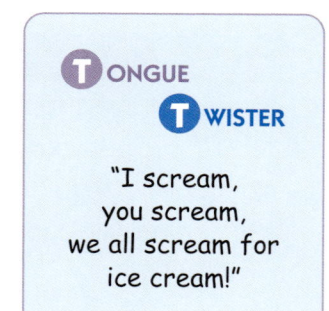

Tongue Twister

"I scream, you scream, we all scream for ice cream!"

---

get used to 〜に慣れる   eventually 結局は、そのうちに   caring 思いやりのある   behavior 態度、ふるまい   warn 注意する

6 FUN TIMES WITH NURSERY RHYMES 🎧 21
Sing with Hand and Body Movements.

「桑の木をまわろう」は、子どもたちの日常の動作をまねながら歌う、楽しい遊戯唄です。まず、手をつなぎ、輪になって歩きながら歌い始めます。"This is the way we wash our hands"「こんなふうに手を洗うのよ」の歌詞のところで止まってそのしぐさをします。「鏡の国のアリス」のなかで、双子のトウィードルダムとトウィードルディーがアリスとこの唄を歌いながら踊る場面があります。

HERE WE GO ROUND THE MULBERRY BUSH

Here we go round the mulberry bush,
The mulberry bush, the mulberry bush,
Here we go round the mulberry bush,
So early in the morning.

This is the way we <u>wash our hands</u>,
Wash our hands, wash our hands,
This is the way we wash our hands,
So early in the morning.

VARIATIONS

You can repeat the verse using other phrases. Choose the correct words and practice the pronunciation of the word pairs.

1. wash our <u>faith / face</u>
2. <u>brush / blush</u> our hair
3. sweep the <u>floor / flour</u>
4. iron our <u>closets / clothes</u>
5. <u>thing / sing</u> a song
6. <u>play / pray</u> the piano
7. <u>walk / work</u> to school
8. _____ (make your own phrase)

mulberry bush 桑の木

5 PANCAKE DAY
"Yum, Yum, Yummy!"

1 JUDGING FROM PICTURES Pancake Recipe

Look at the recipe. Then read the questions and discuss the answers.

a) What ingredients and kitchen utensils do you need to make pancakes?
b) How do you know when it's time to turn the pancake over?
c) What do you like to put on your pancakes?

PANCAKE RECIPE

Ingredients:

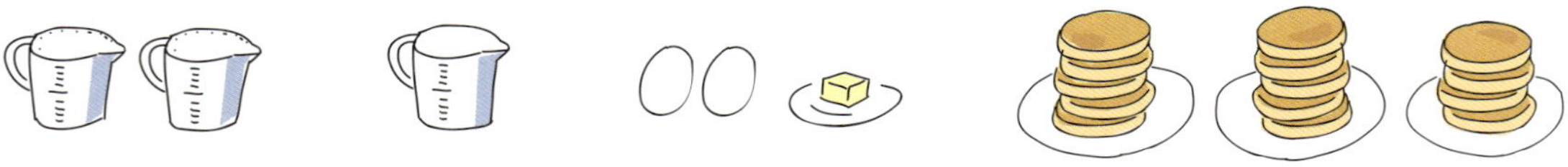

- 2 cups (480ml) of pancake flour
- 1 cup (240ml) of milk
- 2 eggs
- butter

Makes: 14 pancakes

STEPS FOR MAKING PANCAKES

① Mix flour, eggs and milk in a large bowl.

② Heat the pan.

③ Then, spread butter and pour the batter into the pan.

④ Turn pancakes when they become puffy and bubbly. Cook until golden.

⑤ Serve with butter and maple syrup.

---

ingredient 材料　utensil 用具　batter （牛乳、小麦粉、卵などを）こねたもの

2 LISTENING COMPREHENSION The Children Make Pancakes.

Match the English and Japanese expressions.

1. yolk   ____   a. 注ぐ、移す、流す
2. crack   ____   b. 割る、ひびを入れる
3. pour   ____   c. 散らかった、めちゃくちゃな
4. spill   ____   d. 黄身
5. messy   ____   e. こぼす

Listen to the CD and check true (T) or false (F). 🎧 22

	T	F
1. Ms. Ota tells the children to be careful with the pan.	☐	☐
2. Ms. Ota shows them how to fry an egg.	☐	☐
3. Mark drops the eggshell into the bowl.	☐	☐
4. Ana drops the milk bottle on the floor.	☐	☐
5. Soyon helps her mother at home.	☐	☐

3 ADVICE FOR THE INTERNSHIP   Emi's Lecture Notes — Snacks   💿23

Translate the sentences into Japanese.

① Snacks are especially important for young children because their **appetites** (食欲) and stomachs are small.

② Since they can't hold much food at one time, snacks supply the **nutrients** (栄養素) needed for their healthy growth and development.

③ **Exposing** (触れさせること) children to a variety of foods at an early age teaches them to **accept** (受け入れる) more food choices.

TALKING TO CHILDREN
Useful Expressions for Interaction with Children at Snack Time

Translate Japanese sentences into English, arranging the given words.

1. おやつの時間よ。おなかがすいてきたかなあ？(time, it's, empty, your, is, tummy, a, little, snack)

   _____. _____?

2. テーブルの上を片付けて、ふきんで拭いてね。(it, the, table, wipe, with, clear, a, please, cloth, and)

   _____.

3. 今日のおやつは手作りのホットケーキよ。(is, homemade, today's, pancakes, snack)

   _____.

4. 麦茶のおかわりがほしい人はいますか？(wants, tea, more, who, barley, some)

   _____?

4 CONVERSATION Around the Hot Electric Pan 🎵 24

Circle the correct words. Then listen to the CD and practice with your partners.

Emi: Now, who ᵃ**wants to** pour the batter?
Ana: I do, I do.
Mark: No, me first.
Ana: Let's ¹⁾<u>take / talk</u> turns.
Mark: Me first. Oh, look, the batter formed a ²⁾<u>poor / pool</u>. Miss Kato, can I eat this pancake?
Emi: Yes. But remember, we're going to cut all the pancakes in ³⁾<u>have / half</u> and share them with the others.
Ana: Look! There are bubbles. This pancake has become ⁴⁾<u>puppy / puffy</u>. Yummy!
Mark: The edge is getting ⁵⁾<u>dry / try</u>. Yum, yum, yummy!
Emi: Let's turn it over. Oh, it's golden brown. ᵇ**Pass** me the plate, Mark.
Mark: Miss Kato, I want to eat the pancake all by myself. Please.
Emi: No, Mark. Share and share ⁶⁾<u>alike / alive</u>. I know you can.
Mark: Hmm. Then, can I ᶜ**get** two pieces?

SUBSTITUTION DRILL

Use the expressions below to make three more conversations like the one above.

a) Who _____ pour the batter?
b) _____ me the plate, Mark.
c) Then, can I _____ two pieces?

	a	b	c
	wants to	**Pass**	**get**
1	can	Please pass	eat
2	is going to	Can you pass	have
3	is ready to	Will you pass	taste

5 READING AND LISTENING Emi's Journal — Snack Project 🎧 25

Read the journal entry and put in the -ly forms of the words in the box. Then listen to the CD. (See Grammar Notes on page 83)

> final   kind   polite   original   careful   quick

Monday, June 12. Today was Pancake Day. In the morning, the children 1)_____ listened to Ms. Ota and made a shopping list. They listed all of the ingredients needed to make pancakes. Then they talked about where to buy them. 2)_____, they said, "Let's go to the Hungry Kid Supermarket."

At the store the children asked the salesclerks 3)_____ where to find milk, eggs, butter, syrup and pancake flour. At the checkout counter Ms. Ota gave them some money and had them practice paying for the food. The cashier 4)_____ helped them pack their things into the bags. She told them to put the heavy things on the bottom and the fragile things on the top.

Before they cooked, Ms. Ota read them *Pancakes, Pancakes*, a picture book by Eric Carle. From the book, they learned that flour 5)_____ comes from grains, milk comes from cows, and eggs come from chickens. We are so used to getting everything from the store 6)_____, but children have to understand that things are not made at the supermarket.

For the hungry kids, the best part was making their own pancakes, and sharing and eating the yummy treats with their friends.

Which of the answers are correct?

1. At the checkout counter, the children learned...
   a) to put the eggs in the bottom of the bag.
   b) to put the eggs at the top of the bag.
   c) to put the eggs in a separate bag.

2. The book *Pancakes, Pancakes* taught the children...
   a) where food comes from.
   b) the best place to go shopping.
   c) who invented pancakes.

PROVERB

How do you translate the following proverb?

"The best fish swim near the bottom."

fragile 壊れやすい   grain 穀物

6 FUN TIMES WITH NURSERY RHYMES 🎧 26
Recite a Poem and Enjoy a Clapping Rhyme.

19世紀の英国の女流詩人クリスティーナ・ロセッティChristina Rossetti（1830-1894）の詩を聞いてみましょう。この"Mix a Pancake"はシング・ソング童謡集（1872）*Sing-Song: A Nursery Rhyme Book*に書かれた一編です。軽快なリズムを楽しみながら暗唱しましょう。また、赤ちゃんと一緒にケーキを作る手遊び唄も歌ってみましょう。

MIX A PANCAKE

Mix a pancake,
Stir a pancake,
Pop it in the pan;
Fry the pancake,
Toss the pancake,—
Catch it if you can.

PAT-A-CAKE

① Pat-a-cake, pat-a-cake, baker's man,
② Bake me a cake as fast as you can.
③ Pat it and prick it and mark it with <u>B</u>,
④ Put it in the oven for <u>baby</u> and me.

① Help a baby clap his/her hands together to the words.

② Help a baby clap his/her hands faster to the words.

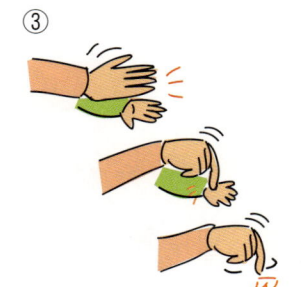

③ Pat the palm of a baby's hand, prick his/her palm with your finger, trace a B on his/her hand.

④ Slide the pretend cake into a pretend oven and point to the baby, then yourself.

VARIATIONS

The "B" and "Baby" in the last two lines are replaced by the child's first initial and first names such as "A" for "Ana," "S" for "Soyon" and "M" for "Mark."

---

pop ポンと置く、ほうりこむ **baker's man** ケーキ屋さん **pat** （手のひらで）たたく **prick** 突く **mark** 印をつける **pretend** see page 46

6 READ ME, TELL ME STORIES
"What Story are You Reading Us?"

1 JUDGING FROM PICTURES The Library Corner

Look at the pictures. Then read the questions and discuss the answers.

a) What are the children going to do?
b) What can you see behind the teacher?
c) What were your favorite books when you were little?

Write the number of each item in the correct box.

| 1. hand puppet | 2. bookcase | 3. mat | 4. pajamas | 5. alphabet book |
| 6. picture book | 7. big book | 8. easel | 9. blanket | 10. picture-card show |

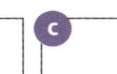

ANSWER: a ☐ b ☐ c ☐ d ☐ e ☐ f ☐ g ☐ h ☐ i ☐ j ☐

2 LISTENING COMPREHENSION Emi Reads to the Children.

Match the English and Japanese expressions.

1. (book)cover   _____   a. 用意、準備ができた
2. ready   _____   b. 注意、注意力、注目
3. attention   _____   c. ガードマン、夜警
4. watchman   _____   d. （本の）表紙
5. stolen   _____   e. 盗む（stealの過去分詞形）

Listen to the CD and check true (T) or false (F). 🎧 27

		T	F
1.	Emi says to the children, "How do you do?"	☐	☐
2.	The children are not sleepy.	☐	☐
3.	Emi has brought a magazine to read.	☐	☐
4.	The children have been to the zoo.	☐	☐
5.	Emi reminds the children to pay attention to the animals in the story.	☐	☐

remind 念を押す、気づかせる

3 ADVICE FOR THE INTERNSHIP
Emi's Lecture Notes — Reading to Children 🎧28

Translate the sentences into Japanese.

① Reading stories can help children **feed their curiosity** [好奇心を満たす] and experience things that won't **come up** [起る] in real life.

② Stories let them develop their language and imagination. Beautiful picture book illustrations teach them about art as well.

③ For a teacher, reading to children is a very special time. Children feel relaxed, **snug and secure** [心地よく、安心して] as they sit on a teacher's lap.

TALKING TO CHILDREN
Useful Expressions for Interaction with Children at Story Time

Translate Japanese sentences into English, arranging the given words.

1. 絵本、読みましょうか？ (book, do, read, me, a, you, to, want, picture)

   _____?

2. おひざに座って。おばけのお話は好き？ (lap, like, sit, do, about, the, story, my, you, ghosts, on)

   _____. _____?

3. 本をやぶかないように、ページはゆっくりめくりましょう。(page, the, gently, book, you, the, turn, so, won't, tear)

   _____.

4. この絵のなかのお花や木をよく見てみましょう。(attention, this, to, in, picture, pay, the, plants)

   _____.

4 CONVERSATION After Reading *Good Night, Gorilla* 🎧 29

Fill in the blanks using the words in the box. Then listen to the CD and practice with your partners.

> Did   Does   How   When   Where   What   Who

Emi: This is the end of the story. 1)_____ you enjoy *Good Night, Gorilla*? Please name the animals you ᵃ**saw** in the story.

Soyon: The gorilla, an elephant, a lion, a hyena, a giraffe and an armadillo.

Emi: That's six. There are seven different animals. 2)_____ anyone remember one more?

Mark: A mouse. The mouse ᵇ**with** the banana! Did he eat the banana?

Emi: Oh, I don't know. 3)_____ is that page? Here it is. There's a banana peel on the bed. 4)_____ do you think? 5)_____ ate it?

Ana: The gorilla. He ate it.

Soyon: No. The gorilla and the mouse shared it. They both ate it.

Mark: No. The zookeeper. He ate it.

Emi: I think he was asleep, Mark. 6)_____ could he eat the banana?

Mark: He wasn't asleep. He pretended ᶜ**to be asleep** and stole the banana.

Emi: Do you think so? Maybe, Detective Mark.

Ana: This is a mystery.

Emi: Well. Thank you for being such good listeners. I enjoyed reading to you. Now go to sleep. 7)_____ you sleep well, you feel great. Bye.

SUBSTITUTION DRILL

Use the expressions below to make three more conversations like the one above.

a) Please name the animals you _____ in the story?
b) The mouse _____ the banana.
c) He pretended _____ and stole the banana.

	a	b	c
	saw	with	to be asleep
1	heard	who has	to be sleeping
2	noticed	who keeps	he was asleep
3	found	who likes	he was sleeping

5 READING AND LISTENING
Emi's Journal — Reading for the Children CD 30

Read the journal entry and circle the correct articles. Then listen to the CD. (See Grammar Notes on page 84)

Tuesday, June 13. I went to the library corner to find a bedtime story. I wanted a book that had beautiful illustrations to amuse the children. ¹⁾ A / The storyline also needed to be simple and nice. At long last, I picked Good Night, Gorilla. ²⁾ An / The author of this book is Peggy Rathmann, who lives in ³⁾ an / the U.S.

Last year, my English teacher read this story to us. At once, it became one of my favorite books. I even ordered ⁴⁾ a / an copy for myself. I discover something new each time I read it. It introduces familiar topics to children, like the zoo and the zoo animals. I thought this was ⁵⁾ a / the right book.

There are few words in this story, but a lot of pictures throughout ⁶⁾ a / the book. I asked the children questions about the pictures before turning the pages. I used different voices for different characters. The children listened and watched carefully. No one stood up or walked around ⁷⁾ an / the entire time. I really enjoyed sharing ⁸⁾ a / the picture book with them.

Which of the answers are correct?

1. What kind of book is *Good Night, Gorilla*?
   a) It's a scientific book for children to study animals.
   b) It's a children's storybook with pictures of animals.
   c) It's a guidebook for a children's zoo.

2. For the children, *Good Night, Gorilla* ...
   a) seemed new and interesting.
   b) was boring to look at.
   c) had an unpleasant ending.

QUIZ

Which words in the story mean the same as:
1. entertain = _____
2. find = _____
3. well known = _____
4. whole = _____
5. choose = _____

---

amuse 楽しませる   at long last どうにか   throughout（本の全ページ）にわたって   entire 全体の、全部の

6 FUN TIMES WITH NURSERY RHYMES 31
Children Have Fun Making Animal Sounds.

「マクドナルドおじさんの農場」には、たくさんの動物がいます。様々な動物の鳴き声やしぐさを楽しみながら歌いましょう。MacDonaldのように"Mac"ではじまる名前はアイルランドやスコットランド系であると言われます。"Mac"は息子という意味で、MacDonaldは a son of Donald、ドナルドさんの息子という意味になります。

OLD MACDONALD HAD A FARM

Old MacDonald had a farm-E I E I O.
And on his farm he had some <u>chicks</u> -E I E I O.
With a <u>chick-chick</u> here. With a <u>chick-chick</u> there.
Here a <u>chick</u>, there a <u>chick</u>. Everywhere a <u>chick-chick</u>.
Old MacDonald had a farm-E I E I O.

VARIATIONS

Repeat the verse using another animal instead of the <u>chick</u>, singing the animal sound.

Animal	Animal Sound
duck	quack-quack
cow	moo-moo
turkey	gobble-gobble
pig	oink-oink
donkey	hee-haw

Match mother animals with baby animals.

Mothers　　　　　　　　　　**Babies**

A. chicken　____　　a. puppy

B. duck　____　　b. lamb

C. dog　____　　c. chick

D. cat　____　　d. kitten

E. sheep　____　　e. calf

F. cow　____　　f. duckling

7 ACTIVITIES WITH WATERMELONS
"A Watermelon Grows in My Tummy."

1 JUDGING FROM PICTURES   Arts and Crafts for All Seasons

Look at the pictures. Then read the questions and discuss the answers.

a) Where did you make seasonal handicrafts when you were little?
b) Have you made any of these items? What are they made of?
c) Which season or which month do you like the best? Why?

Write the number of each handicraft in the correct box next to the month.

1. snowman	2. watermelon slice	3. father's day tie	4. Tanabata ornaments
5. Hina dolls	6. carp streamers	7. collage of leaves	8. moon-viewing dumplings
9. kite	10. flower crown	11. demon mask	12. trick-or-treat bag

January ☐   February ☐   March ☐   April ☐

May ☐   June ☐   July ☐   August ☐

September ☐   October ☐   November ☐   December ☐

2 LISTENING COMPREHENSION Emi Observes Ladybug Fours.

Match the English and Japanese expressions.

1. shape   _____   a. 果肉
2. oval   _____   b. 種、種子
3. flesh   _____   c. 縞、筋
4. stripe   _____   d. 形、形状、外形
5. seed   _____   e. 卵形のもの、楕円形のもの

Listen to the CD and check true (T) or false (F). 32

　　　　　　　　　　　　　　　　　　　　　　　　　　　　T　F

1. Ms. Tano covers a watermelon with a handkerchief.　☐　☐
2. She talks about the size and shape of the watermelon.　☐　☐
3. Hal's father plants watermelons every year.　☐　☐
4. The children cut the watermelon into slices.　☐　☐
5. The outside of the watermelon has dark gray stripes.　☐　☐

3 ADVICE FOR THE INTERNSHIP
Emi's Lecture Notes — Art Activities 🎧 33

Translate the sentences into Japanese.

① Children can express their ideas and feelings through works of art. There is no right or wrong in making art.

② Making art **expands**(広げる) their imagination and **stimulates**(刺激する) creativity. It also develops **eye-hand coordination**(目と手の協応動作).

③ Art activities are **open-ended**(際限のない) activities. Children are more interested in the process than in the product they create.

TALKING TO CHILDREN
Useful Expressions for Interaction with Children Playing with Mud

Translate Japanese sentences into English, arranging the given words.

1. 今度は何を作っているの？ (time, you, this, are, making, what)

   _____?

2. どんな味のアイスクリームかなあ？お味見させてね。(is, taste, this, let, what, it, one, flavor, me)

   _____? _____.

3. 2つの味を作ったのね。：バニラとチョコ。(two, vanilla, you've, and, prepared, flavors, chocolate)

   _____: _____.

4. わあ、それは冷たくておいしそう。(tasty, look, does, cold, and, wow, that)

   _____.

4 CONVERSATION About Watermelons 🎧 34

Circle the correct words. Then listen to the CD and practice with your partners.

Tano: Why don't we eat watermelon seeds?

Akane: Watermelon seeds ᵃ**taste bad** ¹⁾<u>and / but</u> I don't like them.

Tano: I see. What happens if you eat the watermelon seeds?

Hal: A watermelon grows in my tummy and comes out through my belly button.

Tano: Hmm. Actually, if you eat the seeds, they'll come out when you ᵇ**go to the bathroom**. So don't worry, ²⁾<u>and / but</u> it's better not to eat the seeds. Do you understand?

Children: Yes, Ms. Tano.

Tano: OK, children, now you can come ³⁾<u>and / but</u> look at the watermelon slices.

Hal: Can we eat them?

Tano: Good question. You can, ⁴⁾<u>and / but</u> not now; We have to wait till snack time. Take a good look at the slices, then go back to your seats ⁵⁾<u>and / but</u> start drawing. Use the ᶜ**crayons** on your tables.

SUBSTITUTION DRILL

Use the expressions below to make three more conversations like the one above.

a) Watermelon seeds _____.

b) Actually, if you eat the seeds, they'll come out when you _____.

c) Use the _____ on your tables.

	a	b	c
	taste bad	go to the bathroom	crayons
1	look ugly	go to the restroom	drawing paper
2	are hard	go to the toilet	colored pencils
3	smell bad	go potty	paints

5 READING AND LISTENING

Emi's Journal — Make-Believe and Reality 🎧 35

Read the journal entry and circle the correct words. Then listen to the CD. (See Grammar Notes on page 78)

Wednesday, June 14. Today I observed Ladybug Fours Class. In the morning, the children were making mud cupcakes with their little ¹⁾<u>fingers / toes</u> in the sandbox. They used leaves, pebbles and twigs as decorations. Afterwards, they pretended to sell the mud pies to each other. The treats sold out in no time and the children happily clapped their ²⁾<u>heads / hands</u>.

At nap time, Akane asked me to stay beside her. She closed her ³⁾<u>mouth / eyes</u> and I gently patted her ⁴⁾<u>chin / back</u> to put her to sleep. After their nap, the children drew watermelons. One girl couldn't draw at all and was crying. She covered her ⁵⁾<u>face / feet</u> with her little ⁶⁾<u>hands / teeth</u>. I felt sorry for her. I wondered if I should help her, but Ms. Tano said I should not.

When Hal finished drawing, he lowered his ⁷⁾<u>nose / cheek</u> to the top of the picture to smell it and stuck out his ⁸⁾<u>lips / tongue</u> to lick it. He said, "This watermelon is yummy." I could hardly believe my ⁹⁾<u>ears / eyeballs</u>. Later, Ms. Tano told me that Hal didn't actually lick it, but only pretended to. I understood that he had tasted his 'pretend' watermelon in his imagination.

Which of the answers are correct?

1. What did the children in the sandbox do?
   a) They took turns throwing mud cupcakes at each other.
   b) They decorated themselves with leaves, pebbles and twigs.
   c) They enjoyed playing with mud and creating make-believe plays.

2. How did Emi feel when she saw a girl crying?
   a) Emi felt proud of her and wanted to praise her.
   b) Emi felt angry at her and wanted to scold her.
   c) Emi felt sad and wanted to do something for her.

Where is the joke?
"Why is six afraid of seven?"

"Because seven ate nine."

---

make-believe（子どもの遊びなどでの）まねごと、ごっこ　sell out 売り切る　in no time たちまち
stick out 突き出す　pretend（形）想像上の、架空の、うそっこの

6 FUN TIMES WITH NURSERY RHYMES 🎧 36
Enjoy Catchy Counting Rhymes.

子どもたちに数を教えるとき歌う、数え唄を覚えましょう。指を数えながら遊びます。

ONE TWO THREE FOUR FIVE

One, two, three, four, five,
Once I caught a fish alive.
Six, seven, eight, nine, ten,
Then I let him go again.

Why did you let him go?
Because he bit my finger so.
Which finger did he bite?
This little finger on the right.
Ouch!

TWO LITTLE SAUSAGES

① Two little sausages
① Frying in a pan,
② One went, "Pop!"
③ And the other went, "Bam!"

①
Point index fingers up and rock them from side to side.

②
Clap hands upward on "Pop".

③
Clap hands downward on "Bam".

8 HAPPY BIRTHDAY!
"A Star Was Born."

1 JUDGING FROM PICTURES The Celebration Begins.

Look at the pictures. Then read the questions and discuss the answers.

a) What can you see? What is going on here?
b) How do the children look?
c) When is your birthday? Did you have birthday parties at preschool?

Write the number of each item in the correct box.

1. birthday banner	2. streamer	3. birthday hat	4. candle	5. birthday card
6. birthday crown	7. paper cup	8. paper plate	9. cupcake	10. handprint

ANSWER: a ☐ b ☐ c ☐ d ☐ e ☐ f ☐ g ☐ h ☐ i ☐ j ☐

48

2 LISTENING COMPREHENSION Emi Asks about Birthday Parties.

Match the English and Japanese words.

1. celebrate   _____   a. 〜を準備する、用意する、支度する
2. ornament   _____   b. 証明書、免許状
3. hang   _____   c. 飾り、装飾
4. certificate _____   d. 〜をつるす、〜を掛ける
5. prepare   _____   e. 祝う

June 9, 20...

Dear Mr. and Mrs. Wilson,

    We will celebrate Ana's birthday on Friday, June 16, during afternoon snack time in class. Parents and brothers and sisters are welcome to join the birthday party. Parents may contribute cupcakes or homemade cookies for the whole class. We have 20 children in our Butterfly Fives class. Please do not bring in ice cream.
    If you do not want us to celebrate your child's birthday, please let us know a.s.a.p.

Sincerely yours,
Sandy Ota
Butterfly Fives Teacher

Listen to the CD and check true (T) or false (F). 🎵 37

	T	F
1. Emi learns how to celebrate her birthday at the school.	☐	☐
2. The birthday child's family can't join the class party.	☐	☐
3. The birthday crown has a number on it.	☐	☐
4. Ms. Ota gives a birthday child a toy as a birthday gift.	☐	☐
5. Usually, the parents prepare cupcakes and candles.	☐	☐

a.s.a.p. = as soon as possible

3 ADVICE FOR THE INTERNSHIP
The Philosophy of Children's Garden — Celebrations 🎧 38

Translate the sentences into Japanese.

① We celebrate the child's birthday in an age-**appropriate** [適切な、ふさわしい] way during afternoon snack time in the classroom.

② The celebration is purposely kept simple and **child-centered** [子ども主体の]. **Siblings** [(男女の別なく)きょうだい] and parents can join the birthday party.

③ Parents may bring in cupcakes or cookies. They can check with their child's teacher **regarding** [〜について] any food **allergies** [アレルギー] that other children in the class may have.

TALKING TO CHILDREN
Useful Expressions for Interaction with Children about Their Birthdays.

Translate Japanese sentences into English, arranging the given words.

1. アナちゃん、あなたは今日お誕生日ね。おめでとう！(birthday, congratulations, girl, the, you're, Ana)

   _____. _____!

2. さくらちゃんのお誕生日は2月ではなくて3月だね。(February, in, birthday, is, but, Sakura's, March, not)

   _____.

3. ヨンジュンちゃんのお誕生日は2003年8月15日よ。(Yong Joon, was, 2003, August, on, born, 15)

   _____.

4. アンディちゃんはもうすぐ4歳になるね。(four, going, to, is, turn, Andy, soon)

   _____.

4 CONVERSATION Welcoming Mrs. Wilson, Ana's Mother ♪39

Circle the correct words. Then listen to the CD and practice with your partners.

Ota: Children, ᵃ⁾**please welcome** Mrs. Wilson, Ana's mother. She's ¹⁾made / baked the sweets on your tables. Can you say thank you?

Children: Thank you, Mrs. Wilson.

Mrs. Wilson: You're welcome. Thank you for ²⁾having / inviting me today.

Children: Are you one? No. Are you two? No. Are you three? No. Are you four? No. Are you five? No. Are you six? Yeah! ♪ Happy Birthday to You...

Ota: Congratulations, Ana! Six years old! Make a wish and blow out the candle.

Ana: Yay!

Mark: What did you wish?

Mrs. Wilson: ³⁾Zip / Lock your lips, Ana. It's a secret.

Ota: Mrs. Wilson, could you ⁴⁾talk / tell us about Ana when she was a little baby?

Mrs. Wilson: I'd love to. You see, when she was born, her father said...

Ana: Daddy said, "ᵇ⁾**A star** was born." Right?

Mrs. Wilson: Yes, that's right. Ana was such a good, ⁵⁾healthy / heavy baby girl. She slept well and ate a lot. Her first word was "ᶜ⁾**banana**."

SUBSTITUTION DRILL

Use the expressions below to make three more conversations like the one above.

a) Children, _____ Mrs. Wilson, Ana's mother.

b) Daddy said, "_____ was born."

c) Her first word was "_____."

	a	b	c
	please welcome	A star	banana
1	please meet	A princess	dada
2	this is	An angel	mama
3	here comes	A little flower	hi

51

5 READING AND LISTENING — Emi's Journal — Birthday Present 🎧 40

Read the journal entry and put in the comparative -er forms of the adjectives in the box. Then listen to the CD. (See Grammar Notes on page 82)

| old | easy | smart | much | high |

Friday, June 16. Today was interesting for several reasons. First, it was Ana's sixth birthday. Her Mom brought her favorite banana cup cakes. We had a lovely party with the whole class. I didn't tell anyone, but she and I share the same birthday. What a happy coincidence!

Second, there was a new student teacher, Yuta Endo, who started today. I couldn't believe my eyes when I saw him. I first met him in English night class when I was in high school. I liked him then, but we were too shy to talk. He moved up to a 1)_____ level class soon after that.

Three years have passed since then. This time we had a nice little talk. He has become 2)_____ to speak to, and his new glasses make him look 3)_____. Yuta said, "You should give me some advice since you started the internship 11 days before me." I replied, "Well, actually you should know 4)_____ because you're one year 5)_____ than me. Just kidding!" We had a good laugh.

Yuta majors in Social Welfare and hopes to work in the child welfare field as a social worker. I hope we can support and encourage each other as we both have a serious interest in a child-related career. Our reunion is definitely one of the best birthday presents I've ever had.

Which of the answers are correct?

1. Which was true when Emi and Yuta were high school students?
    a) Emi spoke English better than Yuta.
    b) Yuta was better at English than Emi.
    c) Yuta and Emi stayed in the same English class for three years.

2. Today Emi was most excited by ...
    a) the fact that She and Ana share the same birthday.
    b) the fact that She met Yuta again by chance.
    c) the fact that Yuta had broken up with his girlfriend.

Did you know?
In America, a favorite game at children's birthday parties is "pin-the-tail-on-the-donkey." See page 56.

---

coincidence 偶然の一致   have a good laugh 大笑いする   social welfare 社会福祉   -related 〔複合語で〕…と関係のある   definitely 確かに

6 FUN TIMES WITH NURSERY RHYMES 🎵 41
Enjoy Rhymes about Birthdays and Family.

なわとび唄を覚えましょう。2人がこの唄を唱えながら縄をまわします。まわし手は徐々にそのスピードを上げます。跳んでいる子どもたちは自分のお誕生月がきたら、縄から出ます。また、母の日など家族のために子どもたちがお披露目できる手遊びも覚えましょう。

APPLES, PEACHES

Apples, peaches, pears and plums,
Tell me when your birthday comes.
January, February, March, April,
May, June, July, August,
September, October, November, December.

MOTHER'S KNIVES AND FORKS

① Here are mother's knives and forks.
② Here is father's table.
③ Here is sister's looking glass.
④ Here is baby's cradle.

① Hands are placed back to back, fingers interlaced upwards.
② Turn over the hands, fingers still interlaced.
③ Raise index fingers, touching up high.
④ Raise little fingers, touching up. Keep index fingers up.

looking glass 鏡　cradle ゆりかご

9 CHILDREN AT PLAY
"Way to Go, Mark!"

1 JUDGING FROM PICTURES Children's Games

Look at the pictures. Then read the questions and discuss the answers.

a) Which games do you play outdoors? Which ones do you play indoors?
b) What were your favorite games as a child? Why?
c) What is "Rock-Scissors-Paper" in Japanese? What beats scissors?

Write the number of each game in the correct box.

| 1. drop-the-handkerchief | 2. cat's cradle | 3. beanbag toss | 4. kick-the-can | 5. hopscotch |
| 6. pin-the-tail-on-the-donkey | 7. tic-tac-toe | 8. spinning tops | 9. peek-a-boo | 10. dress-up |

ANSWER: a ☐ b ☐ c ☐ d ☐ e ☐ f ☐ g ☐ h ☐ i ☐ j ☐

(That's the) way to go! 〈略式〉よし、その調子だ：いいぞ、よくやった

2 LISTENING COMPREHENSION Emi Asks about Child Development.

Match the English and Japanese expressions.

1. expect　　　　　　　_____　　a. 援助、支援、手伝い
2. developmentally　　_____　　b. 比較用語
3. assistance　　　　　_____　　c. 予期する
4. choose　　　　　　　_____　　d. 発達上で
5. comparative terms　_____　　e. 選ぶ

Listen to the CD and check true (T) or false (F). 42

	T	F
1. Five-year-olds can use their hands like a knife and fork.	☐	☐
2. They still need a lot of help to get dressed.	☐	☐
3. They can follow simple rules when playing games.	☐	☐
4. They aren't always happy to share their toys.	☐	☐
5. They can compare things.	☐	☐

3 ADVICE FOR THE INTERNSHIP
Emi's Lecture Notes — Traditional Japanese Games 🎧 43

Translate the sentences into Japanese.

① Some of the games in western countries are similar to **traditional** (伝統的な、昔からの) Japanese games.

② *Fukuwarai* is a game similar to "Pin-the-tail-on-the-donkey;" a **blindfolded** (目隠しされた) player pins a tail on the picture of a donkey.

③ *Darumasan ga koronda* is similar to "Red Light, Green Light;" players must **freeze** (動きを止める) when "**It**" (（遊戯の）鬼) says, "Red light." Players who don't stop are out.

TALKING TO CHILDREN
Useful Expressions for Interaction with Children in the Playground

Translate Japanese sentences into English, arranging the given words.

1. もう一度やってごらん。先生（私）のほうにボールを投げてみて。(me, try, throw, once, again, ball, the, to)

   _____ . _____ .

2. 君の番だよ。ボールの横に足を出して。(your, ball, the, turn , beside, it's, step)

   _____ . _____ .

3. 足の内側でボールを蹴ってごらん。(kick, with, foot, the, of, your, the, inside, ball)

   _____ .

4. その調子、よくやったね。君はすごいよ。(proud, go, to, I'm, you, way, of)

   _____ ! _____ !

4 CONVERSATION Ball Games 🎧 44

Circle the correct words. Then listen to the CD and practice with your partners.

Mark: I want to kick the ball. ¹⁾Give / Leave it to me, Mr. Endo.
Yuta: Here you go.
Ana: Mark, stop dribbling. ²⁾Pass / Toss it to me.
Mark: Oh, can't we play soccer? Please! Look, ᵃ**those trees** are our goal.
Yuta: All right, children. Let's play soccer. Can you kick the ball into the goal?
Children: Yeah!
Yuta: OK. ³⁾Lady / Ready, set, go!
Mark: Oh, I missed the ball.
Yuta: ⁴⁾Don't / Never mind. Everyone misses from time to time. Just watch the ball carefully next time you ᵇ**kick** it.
Mark: Right.
Ana: Mark, you can't ⁵⁾rest / test. The ball is coming. Run, run, run!
Yuta: Keep an eye on the ball. Go, Mark, go!
Ana: ᶜ**Way to go**, Mark! You ⁶⁾scored / scared a goal.
Mark: My shoe... Where's my shoe? It's ⁷⁾done / gone.

SUBSTITUTION DRILL

Use the expressions below to make three more conversations like the one above.

a) Look, _____ are our goal.
b) Just watch the ball carefully next time you _____ it.
c) _____, Mark!

	a	b	c
	those trees	kick	way to go
1	those lines	dribble	wow
2	those boxes	get	good for you
3	those poles	pass	nice going

5 READING AND LISTENING Emi's Journal — Little Soccer Players 🎧 45

Read the journal entry and circle the correct words. Then listen to the CD. (See Grammar Notes on page 78)

Monday, June 19. Today Yuta played with the five-year-olds. He had intended to play dodgeball with them, but the children wanted to play soccer instead. Even though they didn't have any soccer ¹⁾<u>equipment / equipments</u>, the children quickly chose a goal and started kicking the ball.

When Mark missed the ball, he dropped his ²⁾<u>shoulder / shoulders</u> and looked embarrassed. Yuta went over and encouraged him: "Everyone misses from time to time. Keep trying. One more ³⁾<u>time / times</u> and you'll have it." Sure enough, Mark scored a goal a few ⁴⁾<u>minute / minutes</u> later.

The kids were very active—running and chasing the ball. They seemed to have a lot of ⁵⁾<u>stamina / staminas</u>, but Yuta didn't forget that proper hydration is very important for children. So he regularly reminded them to drink enough ⁶⁾<u>water / waters</u>. Finally, Ana insisted on giving two ⁷⁾<u>point / points</u> to Mark because he had kicked the ball and his ⁸⁾<u>shoe / shoes</u> into the goal! Generous Ana!

Which of the answers are correct?

1. How did the children start playing soccer?
   a) The children suggested it and Yuta agreed.
   b) Yuta suggested it and the children agreed.
   c) Yuta exchanged the dodgeball for a soccer ball.

2. What did Yuta say about drinking water?
   a) "If you drink during the game, you'll get thirstier."
   b) "Let's have a short break. Go and drink some water."
   c) "Let's not drink water. Wait until the game is over."

PROVERB

How do you translate the following proverb?

"Every failure is a stepping stone to success." Do you agree?

---

sure enough 実際に、案の定   proper 適当な   hydration 水分補給   regularly 一定の間隔で   insist on 主張する

6 FUN TIMES WITH NURSERY RHYMES 🎵 46
What Time Was It When the Mouse Ran Down?

Hickory, dickory, dockは古いゲール語で羊を数えるときに使われた数詞の8、9、10に由来するという説が有力です。唄のなかでは、時計の振り子の音を表わしています。ねずみも登場する楽しい手遊び唄です。

HICKORY DICKORY DOCK

① Hickory Dickory Dock,
② The mouse ran up the clock.
③ The clock struck <u>one</u>,
④ The mouse ran down,
① Hickory Dickory Dock.

① Place palms together, rock them from left to right.
② Wiggle fingers upward.
③ Clap hands above head.
④ Wiggle fingers downward.

VARIATIONS

You can repeat the verse changing the time (one to twelve) and clap hands according to what time it is.

QUIZ

What is the Japanese title for *The Ugly Duckling*? Who is the author?:
a) Hans Christian Andersen
b) The Brothers Grimm
c) Aesop

10 BABY NEWS
"May I Change Her Diaper?"

1 JUDGING FROM PICTURES Babies

Look at the pictures. Then read the questions and discuss the answers.

a) What are these babies doing? Have you ever fed a baby?
b) Did your mother give you breast milk or bottle milk?
c) At what age does a baby start to walk?

Write the number of each activity in the correct box.

1. sitting on the potty	2. standing	3. looking in a mirror	4. getting a bath	5. crying
6. playing peek-a-boo	7. crawling	8. holding a bottle	9. waving bye-bye	10. sitting up

ANSWER: a ☐ b ☐ c ☐ d ☐ e ☐ f ☐ g ☐ h ☐ i ☐ j ☐

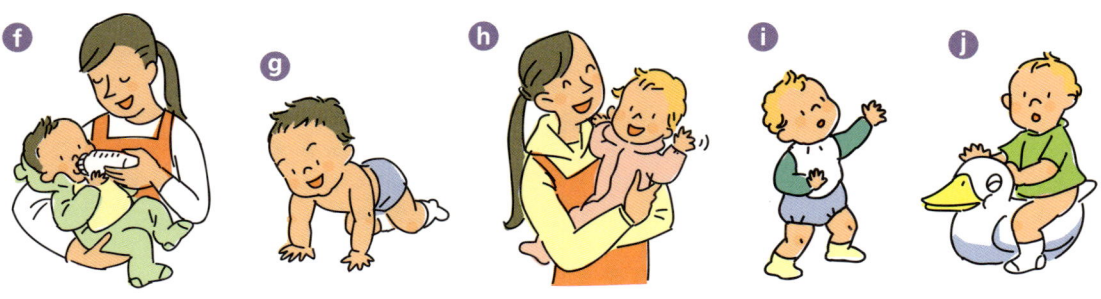

---

fed〔feedの過去形・過去分詞形〕（赤ちゃんに）授乳する   breast milk 母乳   bottle milk 人工乳

2 LISTENING COMPREHENSION Emi Learns about Bambi Babies.

Match the English and Japanese words.

1. information   _____   a. 布おむつ
2. diaper rash   _____   b. おむつかぶれ
3. cloth diaper   _____   c. 歯が生る
4. pick up   _____   d. 知らせること、情報
5. cut a tooth/teeth _____   e. 迎えに行く

Listen to the CD and check true (T) or false (F). 47

	T	F
1. There are nine babies in Miss Ito's class.	☐	☐
2. Emi writes down things she needs to know about the class.	☐	☐
3. Lucy is a new baby who gets diaper rash.	☐	☐
4. Judy's father comes to pick her up today.	☐	☐
5. Ben has started to stand up.	☐	☐

3 ADVICE FOR THE INTERNSHIP
Emi's Lecture Notes — Caring for Infants 🎧 48

Translate the sentences into Japanese.

① Babies do not use words, but they communicate with facial expressions, cries, sounds or body movements.

② **Caregivers** [世話をする人(ここでは保育者)] should always ask themselves what babies are trying to say and **respond** [応答する、答える] to their signals.

③ They may respond by **imitating** [まねること] the sounds babies make or by talking about their needs or feelings.

TALKING TO CHILDREN
Useful Expressions for Interaction with Babies on the Changing Table

Translate Japanese sentences into English, arranging the given words.

1. おむつを替える間、ガラガラで遊んでいてね。(I, with, diaper, a, while, rattle, change, your, play)

   _____.

2. おしりを拭くね。待っててね。(on, bottom, hold, I'll, your, wipe)

   _____. _____.

3. さあ、すごくきれいになったよ。(clean, now, nice, and, you're)

   _____.

4. もうすぐおむつがとれるかなあ。(diapers, of, will, soon, out, I, you, be, think)

   _____.

changing table おむつ交換台

4 CONVERSATION Diaper Change 🎧 49

Circle the correct words. Then listen to the CD and practice with your partner.

Ito: Lucy, why are you crying? Are you wet or ¹⁾<u>angry / hungry</u>? Let me check.

Emi: Oh, ᵃ**she's wet**. May I change her diaper?

Ito: Yes, please. After you wash your hands, make sure you have ²⁾<u>what / that</u> you'll need.

Emi: Of course. A diaper, a diaper cover, and baby ³⁾<u>pipes / wipes</u>.

Ito: That's right. ⁴⁾<u>Lie / Lay</u> the baby down on the changing table.

Emi: OK, Lucy. Let's get you changed. Be still while I ⁵⁾<u>buckle / tackle</u> you in.

Ito: Good. Safety comes ⁶⁾<u>fast / first</u>. Remove the ᵇ**wet** diaper now.

Emi: OK. Now I will wipe her bottom.

Ito: OK. Next, ⁷⁾<u>place / space</u> the clean diaper under the baby.

Emi: There, you're ᶜ**all clean**. Are you happy, Lucy?

SUBSTITUTION DRILL

Use the expressions below to make three more conversations like the one above.

a) Oh, _____.

b) Remove the _____ diaper now.

c) There, you're _____.

	a	b	c
	she's wet	wet	all clean
1	she's dirty	old	nice and clean
2	she needs changing	dirty	clean and dry
3	she needs a diaper change	soiled	nice and clean and dry

赤ちゃん用品の表現：**disposable diaper** 紙おむつ　**diaper cover** おむつカバー　**baby wipes** 赤ちゃん用おしり拭き　**baby bottle** 哺乳瓶　**formula** 調合乳　**baby food** 離乳食　**pacifier** おしゃぶり

5 READING AND LISTENING   Emi's Journal — Real Babies   🎧 50

Read the journal entry and circle the correct words. Then listen to the CD. (See Grammar Notes on page 81)

Tuesday, June 20. As soon as I entered the nursery, a baby boy in a high chair began to cry at the sight of me. I tried 1) <u>to appease / appeasing</u> him by making funny faces. Miss Ito eventually calmed him by calling his name. He soon stopped 2) <u>to cry / crying</u> and allowed me 3) <u>to pick / picking</u> him up.

Holding babies was a bit scary, but exciting. Changing a diaper was challenging though. Lucy didn't stay still on the changing table. I also fed her with the baby bottle. When I put the nipple in her little mouth, she sucked so hard that I was afraid it might pop out. After nursing, I learned how 4) <u>to burp / burping</u> her.

Ten-month-old Matt became quite attached to me. He crawled after me, reached out his hand and cried for me. I couldn't help 5) <u>to hold / holding</u> him tight. He didn't want me 6) <u>to leave / leaving</u> the room without him. I took him for a walk in the stroller. Then I carried him on my back in a sling until he fell asleep. I placed him gently into the crib.

At college, when we studied baby care for infants, we only practiced diaper changes or bottle-feeding with baby dolls. Today I enjoyed 7) <u>to be / being</u> around "real" babies for the first time in my life.

Which of the answers are correct?

1. How did Lucy drink the milk bottle?
    a) She was hardly sucking it.
    b) She was sucking it strongly.
    c) She was noisily sucking it.

2. What did Emi do with Matt?
    a) They went outdoors for fresh air.
    b) They took a nap in the crib.
    c) They carried a sling back to the nursery.

DID YOU KNOW?

Newborn babies don't have tears. Babies begin to have tears when they are about two or three months old.

---

nursery 乳児室   appease なだめる   nipple 哺乳瓶の乳首   (be) attached to 〜になついている   stroller ベビーカー   crib （囲い付きの）ベビーベッド   sling おんぶひも

6 FUN TIMES WITH NURSERY RHYMES 🎵 51
Enjoy a Song We Can Sing to a Baby.

英語圏で最も知られている子守唄を歌ってみましょう。メイフラワー号でアメリカ大陸へ渡ったピルグリム・ファーザーズ（清教徒の一団）の一人が、ネイティブ・アメリカンの女性が木の枝にゆりかごをぶら下げて、子どもをあやす様子を見てこの詩を書いたという説があります。

Listen to the CD and choose the correct word from the box.

HUSH-A-BYE BABY

Hush-a-bye ^a 🧺 on the treetop

When the ^b 🍃 blows, the ^c 🧺 will rock;

When the ^d 🌿 breaks, the ^e 🧺 will fall,

And down will come ^f 👶, ^g 🧺 and all.

1. baby	2. cradle
3. bough	4. wind

ANSWER:

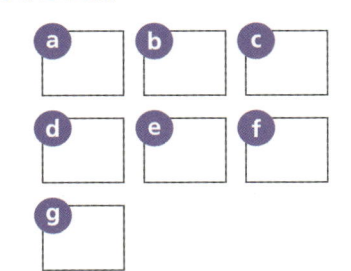

a ☐ b ☐ c ☐
d ☐ e ☐ f ☐
g ☐

PEEK-A-BOO TOY CUP
A Simple Toy to Make and Fun to Play with!

Read the instructions and make your own peek-a-boo toy.

What you need:
1. Two paper cups
2. Colored pencils or felt pens

Instructions:
1. Draw (or glue) a picture of a face on the cup.
2. Cover the face with the other cup.
3. Finished!

How to play peek-a-boo with a baby:
1. Place the peek-a-boo toy cup in front of the baby's face.
2. Lift the covering cup slowly, saying, "Peek-a, peek-a…"
3. Remove it completely and say, "Peek-a-boo. I see you."

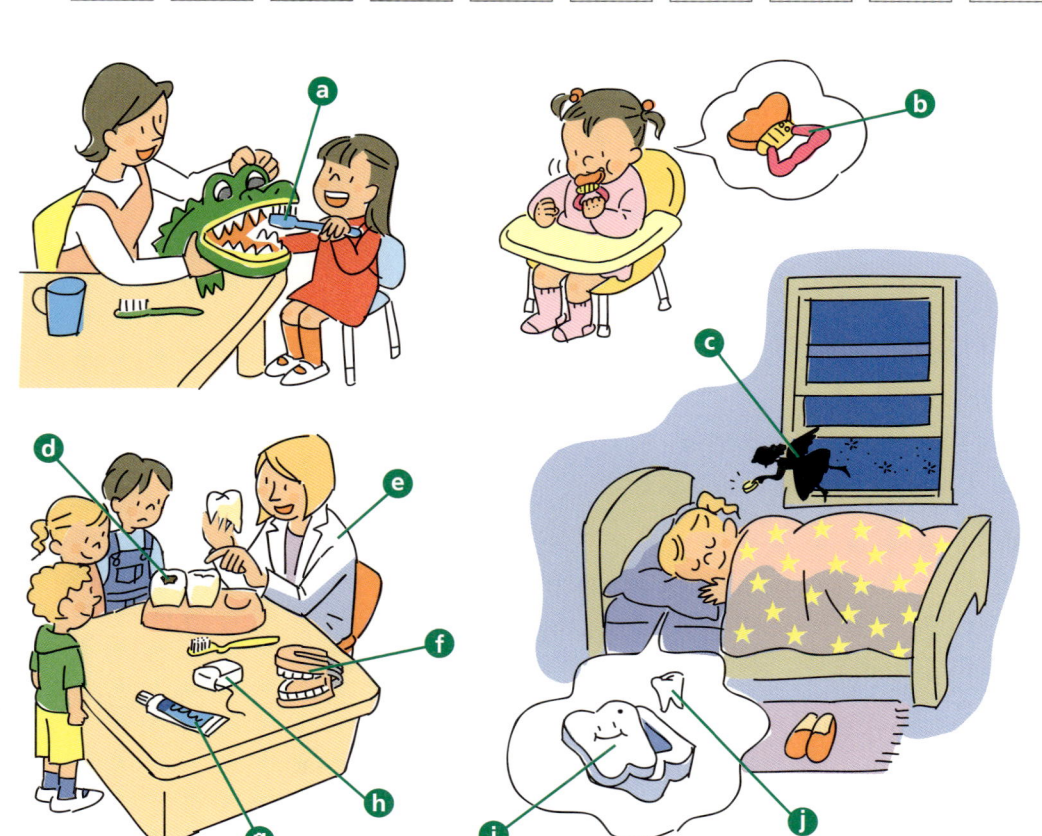

11 THE TOOTH FAIRY
"She Leaves Money under the Pillow."

1 JUDGING FROM PICTURES Dental Health

Look at the pictures. Then read the questions and discuss the answers.

a) What foods are bad for your teeth?
b) How often do you go to the dentist?
c) What do you use to clean your teeth?

Write the number of each item in the correct box.

| 1. tooth model | 2. dentist | 3. teething toy | 4. cavity | 5. toothpaste |
| 6. toothbrush | 7. tooth fairy | 8. baby tooth | 9. floss | 10. tooth box |

ANSWER: a ☐ b ☐ c ☐ d ☐ e ☐ f ☐ g ☐ h ☐ i ☐ j ☐

66

2 LISTENING COMPREHENSION Show Me Your Smiles!

Match the English and Japanese expressions.

1. a thousand times _____   a. 2回、2倍に
2. at least _____   b. 自身の
3. twice _____   c. 各自／めいめいに
4. each (pron./ adv.) _____   d. 1000回、何度も（繰り返して）
5. own _____   e. 少なくとも

Listen to the CD and check true (T) or false (F). 52

	T	F
1. All the children brush their teeth every morning.	☐	☐
2. Ms. Ota checks their teeth by asking them to smile.	☐	☐
3. Mark does not brush his teeth after lunch.	☐	☐
4. Ms. Ota says we should brush our teeth three times a day.	☐	☐
5. The children must not share toothbrushes.	☐	☐

3 ADVICE FOR THE INTERNSHIP
Emi's Lecture Notes — How Teeth Grow CD 53

Translate the sentences into Japanese.

① Between the ages of four and seven months, the first teeth appear. Teething babies seem to **drool** (よだれが出る) a lot and want to **chew on** (〜をかむ) things.

② By the age of three, most children have all 20 baby teeth. It's important to take care of them as they hold space for **permanent teeth** (永久歯).

③ Around the age of five or six, children start losing their baby teeth. They usually lose the upper front teeth first.

TALKING TO CHILDREN
Useful Expressions for Talking with Children about Teeth

Translate Japanese sentences into English, arranging the given words.

1. 前後に歯ブラシを動かして磨きましょう。(and, back, brush, forth, teeth, your)

   _____.

2. はい、こんなふうに、お口をすすぎましょう。(mouth, like, rinse, just, your, now, this)

   _____.

3. 今晩、枕の下にあなたの乳歯を置いて下さい。(baby, tooth, your, put, the, under, tonight, pillow)

   _____.

4. 目が覚めたら、それがコインに変わっているでしょう。(wake, turned, coin, have, you, a, when, will, into, up, it)

   _____.

4 CONVERSATION Losing a Baby Tooth 🎧 54

Fill in the blanks using the words in the box. Then listen to the CD and practice with a partner.

come	exchange	find	fly	keep	look	say	see

Emi: Ana, what's in the locket you're wearing around your neck? I'm curious.

Ana: This is a tooth box. I 1)_____ my baby tooth in it. It fell out this morning.

Emi: Can I 2)_____ it? Oh, it's so tiny!

Ana: The Tooth Fairy is coming tonight.

Emi: Did you 3)_____ Tooth Fairy?

Ana: She visits sleeping children to 4)_____ baby teeth for coins. She leaves ᵃ**money** under the pillow.

Emi: Have you ever seen her? What does she 5)_____ like?

Ana: She ᵇ**wears a pretty gown**. She can 6)_____ and come through the windows. But the last time I lost a tooth, the Tooth Fairy forgot to 7)_____.

Emi: Did she? Maybe she got lost and couldn't 8)_____ your place, Ana.

Ana: No. Mommy says the Tooth Fairy collects ᶜ**healthy** teeth only. That night, my tooth had a cavity.

Emi: Oh!

SUBSTITUTION DRILL

Use the expressions below to make three more conversations like the one above.

a) She leaves _____ under the pillow.

b) She _____.

c) Mommy says the Tooth Fairy collects _____ teeth only.

	a	b	c
	money	wears a pretty gown	healthy
1	a little surprise	has wings	white
2	a silver dollar	wears a golden crown	shiny
3	a dollar note	wears ballet slippers	good

curious 好奇心が強い   get lost 迷子になる

5 READING AND LISTENING
Emi's Journal — The Last Day of the Internship 🎧 55

Read the journal entry and put in the phrases in the box. Then listen to the CD. (See Grammar Notes on page 85)

| believe in | hold back | look forward to | wake up | reminded me of |

Wednesday, June 21. Ana lost a baby tooth. Thanks to the Tooth Fairy tradition, she seems to 1)_____ losing her teeth. This 2)_____ my own childhood: When I lost a tooth, I threw a lower tooth onto the roof, while I threw an upper tooth underneath the floor. I believed that by doing so, my lower and upper teeth would grow in the right direction.

Ms. Ota also told me about the Sandman, who carries a bag of magic sand and brings good sleep by sprinkling the sand into the eyes of children. The "sleep" in their eyes when they 3)_____ is the "sand" that he used, she said.

As an adult, I know that the Tooth Fairy, the Sandman, the Easter Bunny and Santa Claus don't exist. Children, however, 4)_____ these imaginary figures—it is their privilege and in a way I envy them.

Today was my last day as an intern. I couldn't 5)_____ my tears when I went to say goodbye to the children. They've meant so much to me! I'll never ever forget my happy days at Children's Garden!

Which of the answers are correct?

1. Why do children in western countries believe in the Sandman?
   a) They find his gift under their pillow when they wake up.
   b) There is "sand" in their eyes in the morning.
   c) They have seen him carry a bag of sand.

2. Today was the last day of Emi's internship. How did she feel?
   a) She thought it was time to leave the children.
   b) She found it hard to leave the children.
   c) She was thankful to leave the children.

> **Did you know?**
> **What is the etymology of goodbye?**
> Goodbye is a contraction of "God be with ye (you)."

---

thanks to 〜のおかげで、ために   underneath the floor 縁の下へ   sleep 目やに   privilege 特権
etymology 語源

6 FUN TIMES WITH NURSERY RHYMES 🎵 56
Read and Recite a Fairy Poem in Class.

英国やアイルランドには妖精にまつわるお話、詩歌、言い習わしがたくさんあります。たとえば「そばかすは妖精のキス」「風の中を舞う木の葉の音は妖精が近くにいるしるし」と言います。身近に妖精を感じながら暮らしている様子がうかがえます。妖精の詩を読み、訳してみましょう。

Read this fairy poem and find out what to do if you see a fairy ring or a fairy.

IF YOU SEE A FAIRY RING (Author Unknown)

If you see a fairy ring
In a field of grass,
Very lightly step around,
Tiptoe as you pass;
Last night fairies frolicked there,
And they're sleeping somewhere near.
If you see a tiny fairy
Lying fast asleep,
Shut your eyes and run away,
Do not stay to peek;
Do not tell,
Or you'll break a fairy spell.

Summarize the poem by matching the numbered sentences in column A with the correct answer in column B.

Column A	Column B
1. If we see a fairy ring in the grass,	____ a. we must not stop and look.
2. We should walk quietly as we pass	____ b. so that the fairies won't hear us.
3. The fairies made the ring last night	____ c. or the fairy magic will disappear.
4. If we happen to find a sleeping fairy,	____ d. we should go around it.
5. We had better not tell anyone about it	____ e. when they danced there.

fairy ring 妖精の輪、菌環（きのこなどによって草地にできる輪；妖精のダンスの踊り場とされた）。「シェイクスピアは『夏の夜の夢』の中で、妖精の輪を「緑の上の輪」とよんでいる。（中略）ある人が夕方に妖精の輪の中で過ごしたところ、人間の世界では何年も経っていて、帰ったときには家族も家もすでになくなっていた。誰もいない妖精の輪をみつけて中に飛び込むと、若くして死んでしまう。（妖精百科事典）」 **frolick = frolic** はしゃぐ、遊び戯れる、浮かれ騒ぐ

12 THE GREEN-EYED WITCH
"Which Witch Watched Which Watch?"

1 JUDGING FROM PICTURES An Invitation Card

Look at the invitation. Then read the questions and discuss the answers.

a) What is the Butterfly Fives class going to do?
b) What kind of story can you imagine from the title of the play?
c) Have you ever acted in a play? What role did you play?

Dear Parents / Guardians,

The Butterfly Fives is going to present a play next Saturday, December 15. The play is called "The Green-Eyed Witch." The children are acting out a story they created themselves! They have been working very hard for weeks preparing the play.

It is great to see your child have fun playing a role. Please plan on attending.

Sincerely yours,
Sandy Ota
Butterfly Fives Teacher

The Green-Eyed Witch
CHARACTERS, in Order of Appearance:
Narrator - Soyon Kim
Prince/Monster - Mark Guthrie
Owl - Xing Guo Zhao
Bear - Daya Chugani
Monkey - Kwan Bae
Snake - Naomi Pemper
Rabbit - Chie Yoshikawa
Witch - Ana Wilson
Tortoise - Mayumi Kanai

2 LISTENING COMPREHENSION Play Script - Act I (In the forest)

Match the English and Japanese expressions.

1. appear   _____   a. 焼きもちを焼く、うらやんで
2. matter (v.)   _____   b. 痛む
3. medicine   _____   c. 問題である、問題となる
4. hurt   _____   d. 登場する、現れる、出現する
5. jealous   _____   e. 薬、薬剤

Listen to the CD and check true (T) or false (F). 🎧 57

	T	F
1. Miss Squirrel isn't feeling well.	☐	☐
2. The Prince sells medicine bottles.	☐	☐
3. The fruits of the Magic Tree are available all year round.	☐	☐
4. The witch is hiding a rock behind herself.	☐	☐
5. She doesn't like the Prince because he has many girlfriends.	☐	☐

available 入手できる、利用できる

3 ADVICE FOR THE INTERNSHIP — Emi's Lecture Notes — Acting Out Plays 🎧58

Translate the sentences into Japanese.

① Children can **try out** different roles by acting in plays. While they express the feelings or thoughts of a character in a play, they develop confidence in expressing their own ideas.

② They practice not only **oral language** but also body movements and facial expressions. Simple costumes, masks and **props** help them to **get into** a character.

③ When they act in groups, they have to listen to each other and cooperate so they can reach a goal. A play teaches them how to **socialize and interact with** others.

TALKING TO CHILDREN
Useful Expressions for Interaction with Children on Their Big Day

Translate Japanese sentences into English, arranging the given words.

1. 上手！ 拍手しましょう。(hand, big, give, a, great, them, let's)

    _____! _____.

2. 誰が王様の役をやるのか教えて。(who, will, me, king, the, play, tell)

    _____.

3. せりふを覚えるのにどれくらいかかったの？ (you, lines, to, how, your, it, long, did, take, learn)

    _____?

4. 緊張しないでね。ちゃんとできるよ。(nervous, can, don't, be, this, you, do)

    _____. _____.

5. 劇が終ったらお辞儀をするのを忘れないでね。(to, when, don't, over, forget, play, the, is, bow)

    _____.

4 LISTENING COMPREHENSION & CONVERSATION
Play Script - Act II (In the witch's house) 🎧 59

Listen to the CD. Choose the character's emotions and write the number in the box. Take on a role and act out the dialogue in a group.

> 1. angry 2. frightened 3. grateful 4. happy 5. wicked 6. proud 7. relieved 8. worried

Narrator: The Green-Eyed Witch has put the Prince under a spell. He has become an ugly monster. He is put in chains and taken to the witch's house.

Witch: ⓐ Abracadabra. Hocus, pocus. Open sesame. I like sashimi. Which witch watched which watch? M-a-g-i-c. Magic. Hee, hee, hee... Prince, you can't talk any more.

Monster: ⓑ Gggggrrr. (In an awful roar. He's struggling to escape.)

Narrator: The animals are very upset.

Rabbit: ⓒ We must help the Prince. What can we do?

Bear: He's under a spell. Oh, what can we do? Think!

Snake: We need the witch's wand to save him.

Monkey: Yes. We'll go into her house and steal her wand.

Owl: ⓓ I know all the witch's magic words to break her spell.

Animals: ⓔ We can save the Prince with the wand and the magic words. Let's go get her!

Narrator: It's dinnertime. The witch is cooking spiderweb spaghetti. Suddenly the animals break into the house. Mr. Monkey grabs the pan and pours the spaghetti over her head.

Witch: ⓕ A-h-h-h-h! Hot, hot, hot. Oh, I can't see. I can't see.

Narrator: Mr. Bear covers the witch's mouth with his paws. Mr. Snake winds himself around her legs. Miss Rabbit kicks her back. Mr. Owl takes the wand, waves it and says the magic words.

Owl: Abracadabra. Hocus, pocus. Open sesame. I like sashimi. Which witch watched which watch? M-a-g-i-c. Magic. Hee, hee, hee...

Monster: Aaaarrrgh.

(A loud boom)

Prince: ⓖ Thank you, my friends. You've saved me. Thank you.

Animals: ⓗ Hip, hip, hurray. The Prince is back! The Prince is back! (Raising a cheer and dancing around) And the witch...

Prince: The witch is gone forever!

(Applause)

5 READING AND LISTENING   Emi's Journal — What a Show!   CD 60

Read the journal entry and circle the correct words. Then listen to the CD.

Saturday, December 15. Six months have passed since I ended my internship at Children's Garden, when I got an invitation to their play! On the night before the big event, I was so ¹⁾**exciting / excited** that I couldn't sleep ²⁾**by / until** 2:00 am.

I saw the children ³⁾**act / acted** out "The Green-Eyed Witch". Ana, ⁴⁾**which / who** played the witch, pressed two green peppers against her eyes when casting her spell. She looked funny and scary at ⁵⁾**a / the** same time. Mark was the prince who was turned into a monster by the evil witch. Xing Guo played the role of ⁶⁾**a / an** owl. As he waved the wand to break the spell, he ⁷⁾**hit / hitted** Mark's head.

Xing Guo said, "Sorry. I didn't mean to." Everyone laughed. Mark ⁸⁾**nearly / near** shouted, "Ouch!", but continued with a growl, "Ow-ou-aaarrrgh." His strong voice and expressive face made him a good actor. We applauded his acting skills.

Everything ⁹⁾**was / were** joyful. All the children acted well and spoke ¹⁰⁾**in / on** a loud voice, even the shy ones. At the end they joined ¹¹⁾**them / their** hands and took a bow. The parents were very proud of their talented children. I realized how ¹²⁾**many / much** I had missed them since last June. Maybe ¹³⁾**some / all** day I'll return to Children's Garden—not as an intern, ¹⁴⁾**but / and** as a teacher.

Which of the answers are correct?

1. What did Ana use to express the witch's green eyes?
   a) She used a kind of natural paint.
   b) She used a kind of tropical fruit.
   c) She used a kind of fresh vegetable.

2. Why did Xing Guo hit Mark on the head?
   a) He just followed the script.
   b) He accidentally hit his head.
   c) He got excited and angry.

3. What did the parents think of Mark's acting?
   a) They thought him wooden.
   b) They found his acting skills very good.
   c) They thought his performance was disappointing.

QUIZ

What does "green-eyed" mean? Choose the correct answer:
a) jealous
b) funny
c) scary

6 FUN TIMES WITH NURSERY RHYMES 🎵 61
Read and Recite a Rhyme for Christmas.

クリスマスに、ジンジャーブレッドクッキーやハウスを作る習慣はドイツからアメリカに伝わってきたものです。ドイツのクリスマス市では、スパイス（生姜、シナモン、クローヴ等）入りのクリスマスクッキーが様々な形や大きさでクリスマスの装飾品として売られています。

THE GINGERBREAD MAN

Smiling girls, rosy boys,
Come and buy my little toys;
Monkeys made of gingerbread,
And sugar horses painted red.

MINI GINGERBREAD HOUSE
A Gingerbread House Is Simple to Make and Tasty to Eat!

Read the instructions below and try making your own little gingerbread house.

What you need:
1. Six graham cracker squares
2. Icing (recipe below)
3. Colorful candies
4. A plastic (pastry) bag
5. Your imagination

How to make icing:

Pour two cups of powdered sugar, one egg white and one teaspoon of lemon juice or vinegar into a bowl. Mix the ingredients and beat with an electric mixer at a high speed for 10-12 minutes. Pour the icing into a plastic bag and cut off one bottom corner.

How to build a house:

Use the icing as glue to assemble the house. Glue four crackers together, forming the four sides of the house. To make the roof, put two crackers together at a 90-degree angle. Place this on top of the house and glue with icing. Decorate the outside of the house by gluing on your favorite colorful candies. Have fun!

---

graham cracker 全粒粉入りクラッカー　icing アイシング、砂糖衣　assemble 組み立てる　angle 角度

GRAMMAR NOTES

名詞 Nouns — Explanations for Chapters 7 & 9

■数えられる名詞
単数形の場合は不定冠詞（a, an）がつく。数詞（one, ten）がつけられる。複数形には、数を表すmany, fewなどがつけられる。

　　普通名詞—ある種類のものに共通した名（egg, girl, holiday）
　　集合名詞—人や物の集合体（class, family, team）

■複数形の作り方

・規則的複数形

語尾	単数形	sのつけ方	複数形	発音
母音字	bee, eye	+ s	bees, eyes	[z]
s, sh, ch, x, z	box, witch	+ es	boxes, witches	[i z]
子音字（無声音）	group, infant	+ s	groups, infants	[s]
子音字（有声音）	frog, school	+ s	frogs, schools	[z]
母音字+ y	day, toy	+s	days, toys	[z]
子音字+ y	baby, fairy	y + ies	babies, fairies	[z]
母音字+ o	zoo, radio	+ s	zoos, radios	[z]
子音字+ o　例外：pianos, photos	potato, tomato	+ es	potatoes, tomatoes	[z]
f or fe　例外：roofs, chefs	shelf, knife	f or fe + ves	shelves, knives	[z]

・不規則的複数形

	単数形	複数形
母音が変化	tooth, foot	teeth, feet
語尾が変化	child, ox	children, oxen
不変化　例外：fish, fruit, foodは単・複同形、異なった種類を表す場合はfishes, fruits, foods	sheep, deer	sheep, deer

■数えられない名詞
常に単数扱いする。不定冠詞（a, an）はつかない。数詞を直接つけない（two cups of coffee, six pieces of cake）。量を表すmuch, littleなどがつけられる。

　　物質名詞 — 形や区切りがはっきりしない物質や材料を表すもの（water, meat, chocolate, butter, air, bread, soap, paper, oil, rice, sand, hair, sugar, salt, snow, flour, wheat, corn）

　　　　　＊量を表すとき、形状、容器、単位を用いて、a ～ of … の形で表すことができる。
　　　　　（a bar of chocolate, a bowl of rice, a meter of cloth）
　抽象名詞 ― 概念、事物の性質を表すもの（stamina, music, fun, beauty, love, happiness, kindness, advice, peace, homework, behavior, information, applause）
　固有名詞 ― 特定の人、事物、場所の名称を表すもの（Ana Wilson, June, Christmas, Children's Garden Nursery School, Japan, the Izu Peninsula, Sado Island, Mount Fuji, Miyazaki Prefecture）
　　　　　＊大文字で書き始める。不定冠詞はつかない。複数形にならない。定冠詞はつくものとつかないものがある。（p85参照）

■数えられない名詞として用いられる集合名詞
常に単数扱いをし、物質名詞と等しい扱いをする集合名詞がある。量を表すmuch, littleなどがつけられ、数えるときは、a piece of ～などの形で表す。（furniture, equipment, clothing, poetry）

動詞　Verbs　Explanations for Chapter 2

■動詞の語形変化
動詞は原形、三人称単数現在形、過去形、過去分詞形、現在分詞形のかたちに変化する。

原形	hit	work	cry	write	teach	sing
三人称単数現在形	hits	works	cries	writes	teaches	sings
過去形	hit	worked	cried	wrote	taught	sang
過去分詞形	hit	worked	cried	written	taught	sung
現在分詞形	hitting	working	crying	writing	teaching	singing

■三人称単数現在形の作り方
一般動詞の現在形は、動詞の原形と同形であるが、主語が三人称・単数のときは、原形に-(e)sをつける。

語尾	原形	(e)sのつけ方	三人称単数現在形
s, sh, ch, x, z	catch, wash, pass, fix	+es	catches, washes, passes, fixes
母音字+y	play, say, buy	+s	plays, says, buys
子音字+y	study, try, carry	ｙ+ies	studies, tries, carries
子音字+o	do, go	+es	does, goes
上記以外	ask, make, ski	+s	asks, makes, skis
例外：haveはhasに変化する			

■過去形・過去分詞形の作り方
動詞の原形に-(e)dをつけて過去形・過去分詞形をつくる規則動詞と、そうでない不規則動詞の2種類がある。

・規則動詞

語尾	原形	(e)dのつけ方	過去形	過去分詞形
e	like, use, agree	+ d	liked, used, agreed	liked, used, agreed
母音字+ y	play, destroy	+ ed	played, destroyed	played, destroyed
子音字+ y	study, try, carry	y + ied	studied, tried, carried	studied, tried, carried
短母音字+子音字*1	stop, drop	+子音字+ ed	stopped, dropped	stopped, dropped
母音字+ r*2	stir	+子音字+ ed	stirred	stirred
*1 短母音字+子音字あるいは母音字+rで2音節以上の語で、最後の音節にアクセントのあるものの場合	occur, omit	+子音字+ ed	occurred, omitted	occurred, omitted
*2 短母音字+子音字あるいは母音字+rで2音節以上の語で、最後の音節にアクセントのないものの場合	offer, visit	+ ed	offered, visited	offered, visited
上記以外	learn, paint hand	+ ed	learned, painted handed	learned, painted handed

・不規則動詞

原形	過去形	過去分詞形	
cut	cut	cut	AAA型（原形・過去形・過去分詞形が同形のもの）
read	read [red]	read [red]	
come	came	come	ABA型（原形と過去分詞形が同形のもの）
run	ran	run	
have	had	had	ABB型（過去形と過去分詞形が同形のもの）
make	made	made	
do	did	done	ABC型（原形・過去形・過去分詞形がみな異なるもの）
eat	ate	eaten	

■現在分詞形の作り方

動詞の原形に-ingをつけて、現在分詞形をつくる。

語尾	原形	ingのつけ方	現在分詞形
e（発音しないe）	come, take, hope	e+ing	coming, taking, hoping
ie	lie, tie, die	ie + ying	lying, tying, dying
短母音字+子音字*1	stop, get, sit	+子音字+ ing	stopping, getting, sitting
母音字+ r*2	stir	+子音字+ ing	stirring
*1 短母音字+子音字あるいは母音字+rで2音節以上の語で、最後の音節にアクセントのあるものの場合	occur, omit, begin	+子音字+ ing	occurring, omitting, beginning
*2 短母音字+子音字あるいは母音字+rで2音節以上の語で、最後の音節にアクセントのないものの場合	offer, visit	+ing	offering, visiting
上記以外	study, enjoy, do, watch	+ing	studying, enjoying, doing, watching

動名詞と不定詞　Gerund & Infinitive　Explanations for Chapters 4 & 10

■不定詞
「to + 動詞の原形」と「toのない動詞の原形」という二つの形がある。「to + 動詞の原形」をとるものは名詞・形容詞・副詞として用いられる。

- 名詞的用法「〜すること」：主語、目的語、補語となる。
  To change a diaper was challenging.［主語］（オムツ替えは難しかった。）
  The animals didn't know what to do.［目的語］（動物たちはどうすればよいのかわからなかった。）
  Yuta's dream is to work in the child welfare field.［補語］（優太の夢は児童福祉の分野で働くことだ。）

- 形容詞的用法「〜するための」「〜すべき」：名詞を修飾する。
  Emi had a picture book to read.（えみは読むべき絵本を持っていた。）
  Mark wanted something to drink.（マークは何か飲み物がほしかった。）

- 副詞的用法「〜して」「〜ために」：動詞を修飾する。
  Emi was happy to see Yuta.（えみは優太に会えてうれしかった。）
  The animals went to the witch's house to steal her wand.（動物たちは魔女の家へ魔法の杖を盗みに行った。）

■動名詞
動詞の原形 + ingの形で使う。同じ形の現在分詞が「〜している」という形容詞の働きをするのに対し、動名詞は「〜すること」という名詞の意味を表わす。文中で主語、目的語、補語として使う。
  Holding babies was scary.［主語］（赤ちゃんを抱っこすることはこわかった。）
  They kept screaming in the water.［目的語］（彼らは水の中で叫び続けた。）
  Emi's dream is working with kids.［補語］（えみの夢は子どもたちを教えることだ。）

＊前置詞のあとに動名詞を続けて、前置詞の目的語として使う場合、不定詞に変えることはできない。
  Ms. Ota told them to take a shower before swimming.
   （泳ぐ前にシャワーを浴びるように太田先生は彼らに言った。）
  Some children made it through without touching her.
   （なかには、先生に触れずに通り抜けた子どももいた。）

■目的語に動名詞をとる動詞とto不定詞をとる動詞

- 動名詞とto不定詞の両方をとる動詞
  like, start, begin, love, intend, continue

- to不定詞をとる動詞
  hope, plan, wish, decide, promise, expect, agree, refuse, choose, desire, learn

- 動名詞をとる動詞
  enjoy, finish, avoid, give up, mind, practice, stop

・動名詞とto不定詞の両方をとるが意味が異なる動詞

forget, remember, regret, try

Soyon forgot to put the goggles on.（ソヨンはゴーグルを装着するのを忘れた。）

Soyon forgot putting the goggles on.（ソヨンはゴーグルを装着しているのに、装着していることを忘れていた。）

Ana tried to catch a butterfly in the park.（アナは公園で蝶を捕まえようと努力はした。）［実際には捕まえられなかった］

Ana tried catching a butterfly in the park.（アナは公園で蝶を捕まえてみた。）［実際に捕まえた］

形容詞、副詞の比較 Comparisons　Explanations for Chapters 1 & 8

名詞の性質や数を説明する語を形容詞という（cute babies, many children, round face, much money）。この形容詞や様態・数量を示す副詞は性質や状態の度合いを示す比較変化をし 原級、比較級、最上級となる。

■規則変化

・単語が1音節および-yで終わる2音節の場合、-erや-estを使う。*

語尾	原級	er, estのつけ方	比較級	最上級
e	large, wise	+ r, + st	larger, wiser	largest, wisest
短母音 + 子音字	hot, big	+ 子音字+ er, + est	hotter, bigger	hottest, biggest
母音字 + y	coy	+ er, + est	coyer	coyest
子音字 + y	happy, pretty	y + ier, y + iest	happier, prettier	happiest, prettiest
上記以外	small, long few	+ er, + est	smaller, longer fewer	smallest, longest fewest

・単語の音節が2音節以上の場合、また、-lyで終る副詞はmoreやmostを使う。

原級	比較級	最上級
careful	more careful	most careful
important	more important	most important
slowly	more slowly	most slowly
easily	more easily	most easily

＊2音節の語で-er, -le, -ow, -ureなどで終わる単語も + er, + estを使う。

■不規則変化

原級	比較級	最上級
good, well	better	best
bad, ill	worse	worst
many, much	more	most
little	less	least

副詞 Adverbs　Explanations for Chapter 5

副詞は、動詞、形容詞、他の副詞、文全体を修飾する。大多数の副詞は形容詞の語尾に-lyをつけて作る。(careful→carefully, final→finally, kind→kindly, nice→nicely, original→originally, quick→quickly, sudden→ suddenly) また、形容詞と同形のものもある。(early, fast, late, long, hard, well)

■語尾を変化させて作る副詞

語尾	形容詞	lyのつけ方	副詞
子音字 + y	easy, lucky, happy, angry	~~y~~ + ily	easily, luckily, happily, angrily
子音字 + le	simple, gentle	~~e~~ + y	simply, gently
-ll	full, dull	+ y	fully, dully
-ue	true, due	~~e~~ + ly	truly, duly

前置詞 Prepositions　Explanations for Chapter 3

前置詞は前置詞 +（代）名詞のまとまりで、形容詞や副詞と同じ働きをする。前置詞そのものは、時、場所、方向、運動などを表す。

■様々な前置詞

The medicine was sent to Miss Squirrel.（お薬はりすさん（に、へ、）まで送られた。）
The medicine was sent for Miss Squirrel.（お薬はりすさんのために送られた。）
The medicine was sent by Miss Squirrel.（お薬はりすさんによって送られた。）
The medicine was sent from Miss Squirrel.（お薬はりすさんから送られた。）

■時を表わす前置詞

at ……… at eight o'clock, at noon/night/midnight ［時間］
on ……… on Sunday, on October 31, on weekends ［曜日と日］
in ……… in November, in 2010, in the summer, in the morning/afternoon/evening ［月、年、季節］
during … Emi called Ms. Ota during the children's nap time. ［期間中］
since　… Three years have passed since then. ［ある時点から継続］

＊this, last, next, everyなどが時を表す語につくと、at, on, inは不要になる。(this afternoon, every night)

■場所、方向を表わす前置詞

Ana found the ladybug in the box (or on the box, under the box, behind the box).（中に、（上に、下に、後ろに））
Ana is running toward Emi.（〜に向かって）
The Sandman sprinkles the sand into the eyes of children.（〜の中に）
The flower shop is between the Hungry Kid Supermarket and the bakery.（〜と〜の間に）

The tooth fairy flies through the open window. （〜を通り抜けて）
Ana was pressing two green peppers against her eyes. （〜に押し付けて、もたれて）
Line up outside the classroom. （〜の外に）
Come inside the classroom, it is cooler. （〜の中に）
Akane slept beside (next to) Emi. （〜のそば（隣）に）
Emi lives in Tokyo. （〜の中に）
Emi lives at 132 Sakuramachi./Emi is at the post office. （〜の中に、inより狭く、小さい場所を表す）

■その他の前置詞
Emi read the story about the zoo. （関連：〜について）
Emi read the story of the gorilla and the watchman. （関連：〜に関しての）
Emi marked her calendar with a red marker. （手段・道具：を使って）
Serve with butter and maple syrup. （随伴：と共に）
Serve without butter and maple syrup. （〜なしに）
Mary looks like her father. （類似：のような）

冠詞 Articles　Explanations for Chapter 6

冠詞は名詞の前に置かれ、不定冠詞a, anと定冠詞theがある。

■不定冠詞 a, an
不特定のあるものを指す。名詞が数えられる名詞の単数形の場合、子音で始まる語の前はa、母音で始まる語の前はanを使い、複数形や数えられない名詞の場合は、無冠詞になる。その場合、不定冠詞の代わりにsomeをつけることがよくある。
Emi has found a good picture book in the library.
Emi has found an old picture book in the library.
Emi has found old books in the library. (*or* Emi has found some old books in the library.)
Mark buys an apple every day.
Mark buys apple juice every day. (*or* Mark buys some apple juice every day.)

■定冠詞 the
はっきり特定できるものを指す。普通名詞、集合名詞、物質名詞、抽象名詞につく。
Emi has found the picture book.
　［えみが見つけた絵本がどの絵本かはっきり認識できる］
Emi has found the picture books.
　［えみが見つけた複数の絵本がどの絵本かはっきり認識できる］
Mark buys the apple.
　［マークがどのりんごを買うのかはっきり認識できる］

Mark buys the apples.
　［マークがどのりんごを複数買うのかはっきり認識できる］
Mark buys the apple juice.
　［マークがどのりんごジュースを買うのかはっきり認識できる］

＊一つの名詞に二つ以上の冠詞または冠詞相当語（one, another, each, every, some, any, either, neither, no / this, that, these, those / my, your, his, her, its, our, theirなど）を並べて用いることはできない。

■固有名詞と冠詞
固有名詞は普通無冠詞であるが、冠詞をつける場合がある。
　　the United States of America, the Philippines, the Alps ［複数形の国名、山脈名］
　　the Shinano, the Pacific Ocean, the Japan Sea, the Kamchatka ［川、海、半島］
　　the White House, the Red Cross Hospital, the Nozomi ［公共の建物、乗り物］

句動詞 Phrasal Verbs　Explanations for Chapter 11

句動詞は、動詞＋前置詞または動詞＋副詞で構成され、群動詞ともよばれ、一つの動詞の働きをする。

believe in ～（～の存在や正当性を信じる）
　　Ana *believes in* the Tooth Fairy.
hold back ～ *or* hold ～ back（動作、状態）を引っ込めておく、押しとどめる、（感情）を抑える
　　Mark couldn't *hold back* his anger and began punching Xing Guo.
look forward to ～（～を楽しみに待つ）
　　Emi is really *looking forward* to seeing the children and the teachers at Children's Garden again.
wake up ～ *or* wake ～ up（起きる、目が覚める、目を覚ます、（人）を起こす）
　　Emi *wakes up* at six o'clock in the morning.
　　Ana *wakes* her parents *up* early on Sunday morning.

REFERENCES

Baring-Gould, William S., and Ceil Baring-Gould. *The Annotated Mother Goose.* New York, NY: Meridian, 1967.

Beall, Pamela, Susan Hagen Nipp. *Wee Sing And Play.* Los Angeles: Price Stern Sloan, 1981.

Carle, Eric. *Pancakes, pancakes!* New York, NY: Simon & Schuster Books for Young Readers, 1990.

Carroll, Lewis. *Through the Looking-glass, and What Alice Found There.* London: Macmillan and Co., 1872.

Condon, Camy, ed. *Eigo no Asobi Uta.* Tokyo, Japan: Hyouronsha, 1976.

Delamar, Gloria T. *Children's Counting-Out Rhymes, Fingerplays, Jump-rope and Bounce-Ball Chants and Other Rhythms.* Jefferson, North Carolina: McFarland & Company, Inc., Publishers, 1983.

Delamar, Gloria T. *Mother Goose From Nursery to Literature.* Jefferson, North Carolina: McFarland & Company, Inc., Publishers, 1987.

Franklin, Anna. *The Illustrated Encyclopedia of Fairies.* London, England: Paper Tiger, 2002.

Hirsch, Jr., E.D., and John Holdren. *What Your Kindergartner Needs to Know: Preparing your Child for a Lifetime of Learning.* New York, N.Y.: Dell Publishing, 1996.

Howard, Margaret, narr. *A Fairy Fantasy: Music and Verse of Fairyland.* Audio CD. Classical Communications Ltd., 2005.

Opie, Iona Archibald, and Peter Opie. *The Oxford Dictionary of Nursery Rhymes.* Oxford: Oxford University Press, 1951.

Opie, Iona Archibald, and Peter Opie. *The Oxford Nursery Rhyme Book.* Oxford, New York: Oxford University Press, 1955.

Rathmann, Peggy. *Good Night, Gorilla.* New York, N.Y: Puffin Books, 2000.

Rossetti, Christina. *The Complete Poems.* London, England: Penguin Classics, 2001.

TEXT PRODUCTION STAFF

edited by	編集
Toshiko Kobayashi	小林 トシ子
Erika Tsuneizumi Wiseberg	常泉 絵里香
English-language editing by	英文校閲
Bill Benfield	ビル・ベンフィールド
illustrated & cover design by	イラスト・表紙デザイン
Yoko Sekine	関根 庸子
text design by	本文デザイン
Miyuki Inde	印出 美由紀

CD PRODUCTION STAFF

recorded by	吹き込み者
Carolyn Miller	キャロリン・ミラー
Donna Burke	ドナ・バーク
Joanna Chinen	ジョアナ・チネン
Vicki Glass	ビッキー・グラス
Iain Gibb	イアン・ギブ

Children's Garden
English for Early Childhood Care and Education Majors
保育英語

2009年1月20日　初版発行
2019年3月15日　第13刷発行

著　者　　赤松 直子
発行者　　佐野 英一郎
発行所　　株式会社 成美堂
　　　　　〒101-0052　東京都千代田区神田小川町3-22
　　　　　TEL 03-3291-2261　FAX 03-3293-5490
　　　　　https://www.seibido.co.jp

印刷・製本　　倉敷印刷（株）

ISBN 978-4-7919-1095-3　　　　　　　　　Printed in Japan

・落丁・乱丁本はお取り替えします。
・本書の無断複写は、著作権上の例外を除き著作権侵害となります。